Redleaf *Quick* Guide

Caring for Young Children with Special Needs

Cindy Croft

Redleaf Press®
www.redleafpress.org
800-423-8309

Published by Redleaf Press
10 Yorkton Court
St. Paul, MN 55117
www.redleafpress.org

First edition 2017
Cover design by Jim Handrigan
Cover photo by Jaren Wicklund, Getty Images/iStockphoto
Typesetting by Douglas Schmitz
Typeset in Signo and Avenir
Printed in the United States of America

Library of Congress Cataloging-in-Publication Data

Names: Croft, Cindy, author.
Title: Caring for young children with special needs / Cindy Croft.
Description: St. Paul, MN : Redleaf Press, [2017] | Series: Redleaf quick
  guides | Includes bibliographical references.
Identifiers: LCCN 2016028151 (print) | LCCN 2016048243 (ebook) | ISBN
  9781605545042 (paperback : alk. paper) | ISBN 9781605545059 (e-book)
Subjects: LCSH: Children with disabilities--Services for. | Child
  development. | BISAC: EDUCATION / Special Education / General. |
EDUCATION / Inclusive Education. | FAMILY & RELATIONSHIPS / Children with
Special Needs. | EDUCATION / Preschool & Kindergarten.
Classification: LCC HV888 .C76 2017 (print) | LCC HV888 (ebook) | DDC
  362.4083--dc23
LC record available at https://lccn.loc.gov/2016028151

Printed on acid-free paper

U23-02

To the Center for Inclusive Child Care staff, Priscilla Weigel and Dea Anderson, for their passion and commitment to seeing that all children are successfully included in early childhood settings.

To my granddaughter Penelope, who is showing me the wonder and joy of early childhood development all over again.

CONTENTS

INTRODUCTION

Children First

All children are children first. They are children before they are anything else, including the impressions they give one another by how they look, how they learn, or how they act. As caregivers, we need to acknowledge the fundamental truth that all children are worthy simply because they are. Though children are different in many ways, we can honor their differences as well as the similarities that tie them—and us—together.

Young children with and without special needs share many commonalities in addition to their own particular personalities and characteristics. As educators, our work is to celebrate each child as unique and, at the same time, build an ever-adapting early childhood environment that promotes belonging, tolerance, and acceptance. This book will describe specific disabilities and early childhood programming adaptations that address these disabilities. The goal is to guide educators in the philosophy of universal design for learning (UDL). In UDL, the classroom environment is set up so young children can learn through multiple experiences. It is an ongoing, flexible process that constantly adapts to children's learning needs.

Special Needs Defined

When we consider caring for young children with special needs, we first need to understand what is meant by the term *special needs*.

- *Special needs* is a term that can be used to describe disabilities in a broad scope. The Americans with Disabilities Act (ADA) defines disability as anything that interferes with life functions such as learning, speaking, walking, and relating to others (ADA 2009). *Special needs*, defined more narrowly, are assessed disabilities, which have to meet specific medical or educational criteria. For instance, cerebral palsy and Down syndrome are medical diagnoses. Special education law establishes thirteen categories of disability, including learning disabilities and autism.

- *Disability* is a legal term under the ADA, which defines a person with a disability as someone who has a physical or mental impairment that substantially limits one or more major life activity, who has a record of an impairment, or who is perceived as having an impairment (ADA 2009).

Special needs and *disabilities* are terms that will be used interchangeably in this book to refer to conditions that affect a child's learning, development, or relationships with others, especially peers. However they are used, it should be clear to the early childhood educator that disabilities do not define *who* children are. Rather, a disability is an important characteristic of a child, much like temperament or ethnicity. A special need or disability is one thing that makes a child unique, combined with all the child's characteristics.

When we recognize that we all have differing strengths and needs, we can grow toward greater awareness and tolerance of one another and, more importantly, toward acceptance of our differences. This acceptance is especially critical in the early childhood years, when young children are forming impressions of others. For each child, these impressions form an important lens for viewing the world as the child grows into adulthood.

Inclusion

Inclusion means that children with and without special needs are learning, playing, and working alongside one another in the same settings. Inclusion relies on the following ideas:

- Young children learn from one another by being with one another.

- All children must have opportunities to belong—to be integral members of their child care communities.

- Inclusion gives all children the chance to understand others' experiences in ways that help them see that they are truly more alike than different.

The first chapter of this book explains the concept of inclusion in detail. But its foundation is the core philosophy that each child, with or without disabilities, has unique learning needs that can be met through the ongoing adaptations of developmentally appropriate practice and universal design of learning. Inclusion is as much an attitude as it is a practice. When early childhood care providers see a child in the context of the child's wholeness and not just through the lens of the child's disability, they can then see the possibilities in program and activity modifications. Inclusion becomes the lens. It leads providers to ask, "How does my program adapt to meet this child's unique needs while ensuring everyone belongs and feels accepted?" The goal of this book is to give concrete tools for including young children with specific disabilities into high-quality early childhood programming.

CHAPTER 1: THE MEANING OF INCLUSION

Jennifer is a three-year-old with Down syndrome. She has been enrolled in her neighborhood child care center since she was twenty-two months old. When she first started child care, she was reserved and clung to one teacher, Ms. Susan. Now she has made several friends in the preschool room and loves coming in the morning. She is gaining vocabulary as she interacts with peers and a confidence in her own ability to join in play.

Definition of Inclusion

All children, like Jennifer, deserve a sense of acceptance and belonging in their communities. For any child, this means having the same opportunities to participate that others have. These opportunities should focus not on ability or special needs but instead on children's full inclusion in the world around them. Disability laws like the Americans with Disabilities Act protect the rights of all young children to be included in their community child care settings. Beyond legal requirements, inclusion is the best practice for early education programs for the following reasons:

- Years of research support the benefits of high-quality inclusive programs for both children with disabilities and those without disabilities (NPDCI 2011).

- By being in settings with their typically developing peers, young children with disabilities gain many positive outcomes, such as social competencies, better language and communication skills, problem-solving abilities, greater assertiveness, and pride in achievements.

- More than seventy years ago, developmental psychologist Lev Vygotsky believed that the greatest difficulties for children with disabilities came from their isolation from same-age peers rather than their development needs. In his view, young children learn important early skills, particularly language, through social interactions with peers and adults, thus making the inclusive environment a critical learning tool (Berk and Winsler 1995).

- The early years are important times for teaching all young children to honor differences in one another in order to develop a compassionate view of the world.

- Children who are typically developing in programs with a variety of peers who have differing needs learn to accept others as they are, develop patience and compassion, and learn to help others, among other skills (Bentley 2005).

In order to be successful at including young children, we need to understand what the term *inclusion* means. To understand inclusion as a practice in early childhood programs, we can turn to the joint policy statement of the US Department of Health and Human Services and the US Department of Education for guidance. In this statement, inclusion means "holding high expectations [for children with disabilities] and intentionally promoting participation in all learning and social activities, facilitated by individualized accommodations; and using evidence-based services and supports to foster their development (cognitive, language, communication, physical, behavioral, and social-emotional), friendships with peers, and a sense of belonging" (US DHHS and US DOE 2015). Participation, accommodations, and opportunities for friendship and belonging are all hallmarks of high-quality inclusive early childhood settings.

In 2009, the National Association for the Education of Young Children (NAEYC) and the Division for Early Childhood (DEC) of the Council for Exceptional Children (CEC) wrote a joint position statement on inclusion in early childhood. It represents a shared national definition of inclusion meant to alleviate the confusion around what inclusion should look like in child care programs. It is important to practitioners because it provides a common ground for conversation about not only what inclusion is but also how it can be successfully implemented. The following is the DEC-NAEYC definition of inclusion:

> Early childhood inclusion embodies the values, policies, and practices that support the right of every infant and young child and his or her family, regardless of ability, to participate in a broad range of activities and contexts as full members of families, communities, and society. The desired results of inclusive experiences for children with and without disabilities and their families include a sense of belonging and membership, positive social relationships and friendships, and development and learning to reach their full potential. The defining features of inclusion that can be used to identify high quality early childhood programs and services are access, participation, and supports (DEC/NAEYC 2009).

The federal policy statement and the DEC-NAEYC position statement echo similar themes around inclusion: participation of all children regardless of ability, supporting young children's developmental gains by providing accommodations in programming and activities, and increasing the sense of belonging for both the child and the family in their community. These are the core values of a high-quality inclusive early childhood setting. They represent a commitment to helping all young children reach their full potential.

Program Philosophies of Inclusion

The DEC-NAEYC position statement on inclusion gives early childhood educators a framework for creating a program philosophy around inclusion. It guides programs to create philosophies that can ensure that "practitioners and staff operate under a similar set of assumptions, values, and beliefs about the most effective ways to support infants and young children with disabilities and their families. A program philosophy on inclusion should be used to shape practices aimed at ensuring that infants and young children with disabilities and their families are full members . . . and have multiple opportunities to learn, develop, and form positive relationships" (DEC/NAEYC 2009). Following are some guidelines to consider when establishing a program philosophy:

- A written philosophy around inclusion should be part of both the family handbook and the materials on staff expectations.

- Written policies around inclusion should align with a program's mission and values statement and should reinforce the importance of building a community of respect.

- Staff members feel supported when they know that the mission of their organization includes a commitment to values that respect the young children and families with whom they work.

- If staff members have clear expectations of their role in working with all children, fewer issues will arise when children are identified as having developmental concerns or when new children with assessed disabilities are placed in their classrooms.

- A written philosophy or policy on inclusion can help prevent confusion among the staff about enrollment of young children with disabilities or expulsion of children currently enrolled.

- Any policy that seems to screen out children with disabilities needs to be carefully examined and rewritten in a way that does not discriminate but creates an atmosphere of acceptance (US DOJ 1997).

- Informing families upon enrollment about a program's policy of including all children can set the tone for a trusting and respectful relationship.

- An inclusion policy that articulates the program's philosophy is also helpful to families of children with and without disabilities if issues around a child's behavior or development arise after enrollment. The policy can be an effective operational tool for early childhood programs.

Practical Application: Making Inclusion Work

Young children have a wonderful ability to adapt and adjust to one another as they learn and play together. For children with special needs, their worlds are opened up and broadened through experiences with other children in natural settings. A natural setting is a typical setting for any child at a given age without a disability. The goal of inclusion is to provide high-quality, enriching opportunities for young children with disabilities in natural settings or environments.

However, there can be challenges to making inclusion work:

- Without a shared vision for inclusion, staff members in early childhood programs can be at odds with supervisors and one another about how to proceed with children's adaptations or what the expectations are for modifying curriculum or activities. Tools like the DEC-NAEYC position statement on early childhood inclusion can guide staff members in defining a philosophy of inclusion for their program. This shared vision sets the groundwork for a written inclusion policy, which can be shared with families as well.

- Staff members may not know how to field questions from families of children without special needs who express concerns over their children receiving less attention if a child with disabilities is enrolled. A shared vision statement of inclusion can guide staff members in making decisions that promote the values of the program.

- Early childhood professionals say they need training and professional development in order to feel equipped to work with children of differing abilities. Resources and supports provided by directors, specialists working with the children, the families, and disability organizations can be tools for staff support.

- Time, energy, and staffing may be challenges to inclusion if organizational supports are not in place for child care providers. In all child care settings, attention must be given to a child's true needs for teacher-child support. Decisions should not be based on assumptions about a particular disability.

- Fear and lack of confidence in providing high-quality care to children with disabilities can be a barrier for child care providers. Ongoing communication with families about what works well for their children at home can be one way to overcome this challenge. Opportunities for discussion with other specialists (with written family permission) can also alleviate caregivers' lack of confidence.

There are also a variety of benefits to making inclusion work. Inclusion can benefit families, children with disabilities, children without disabilities, and child care providers.

Benefits of Inclusion for Families

- Learning to accept their children's strengths and needs

- Sharing common experiences and feeling kinship with other families

- Having the opportunity to see chronologically age-appropriate activities

- Being able to work outside the home thanks to increased access to child care services

- Discovering that others can provide a secure and nurturing learning environment for their children with special needs

- Understanding that all children have negative behaviors such as tantrums or toilet problems, not just their children with special needs

Benefits of Inclusion for Children with Disabilities

- Learning to accept their own strengths and needs
- Noticing similarities among themselves and others
- Making friends
- Learning by imitating others
- Developing better language and communication skills
- Learning to become more assertive
- Showing more pride in achievements
- Building interdependence and the ability to deal with obstacles
- Developing interpersonal skills
- Increasing problem-solving ability
- Learning self-respect by being a part of a positive, natural environment

Benefits of Inclusion for Children without Disabilities

- Learning to accept others as they are
- Developing patience and compassion
- Accepting others as individuals, not labels
- Learning to help others

Benefits of Inclusion for Child Care Providers

- Developing awareness that all people have unique needs
- Expanding their knowledge about children with special needs
- Realizing and appreciating differences
- Developing compassion, kindness, and respect for others
- Creating a setting that encourages understanding and flexibility
- Developing networks of professional services and community resources
- Acquiring a larger share of the child care market by enhancing their provided services

(Used with permission from Bentley 2005.)

CHAPTER 2: DISABILITY LAW AND ITS IMPACT ON EARLY CHILDHOOD PROGRAMS

Jamal is four and has asthma. He is enrolled in a child care center that refused to modify its medication administration policy to meet his medical needs. His parents filed a complaint under the Americans with Disabilities Act, saying that the center was discriminating against Jamal on the basis of his asthma. A settlement agreement under the ADA required the center to adopt a new asthma medication policy that did not exclude a child with an asthma-related disability and to post the new policy where both families and staff members could access it (Child Care Law Center 2011). Jamal was able to stay enrolled in this program.

The Goal of Disability Law

Disability law is intended to help providers and families look at what is reasonable to meet the needs of an individual child with a disability in order to include that child in a program successfully. Disability law includes two types of laws: civil rights laws and entitlement laws. Both types are considered when deciding reasonable accommodations for young children.

The Americans with Disabilities Act

The Americans with Disabilities Act was signed into law in 1990. It is a civil rights law for people with disabilities. It affects child care programs through its Title III, "Public Accommodations and Services Operated by Private Entities." It applies to private child care centers, preschools, and family child care homes not operated by religious entities. The Department of Justice investigates complaints of discrimination under the ADA. Hundreds of legal settlements have been made with child care programs across the United States based on ADA rulings. Most rulings involve additional training for staff members, changes to program policies, and sometimes monetary damages to families.

How the ADA Defines Disability

The definition of a person with a disability under the ADA is broad. It includes the following categories:

An Individual with a Disability. A physical impairment or limitation as defined under the ADA includes many conditions, such as muscular dystrophy, seizure disorder, cerebral palsy, or diabetes. A disability can also be a mental impairment, such as mental illness or behavior disorder.

An Individual Perceived as Having a Disability. If a person is discriminated against because someone believes he or she has a disability, this is also against the law. For instance, a child could not be excluded from a child care program because a teacher heard the child might have autism.

An Individual with a Record of Having Had a Disability. If someone had a disability, such as cancer, but it has been treated successfully, the person cannot be discriminated against based on past history of disability. For example, a child care program could not exclude a child who had a cleft palate that was surgically repaired.

Why the ADA Is Important to Child Care Programs

Generally, the ADA requires that child care programs follow these rules:

- Programs cannot discriminate against young children with disabilities on the basis of their disabilities.

- Programs must give children and families with disabilities equal opportunities to participate in the programs' services.

- Programs must be generally accessible for young children with disabilities unless making them accessible would constitute an undue burden. Constructing a new early childhood site constitutes a different burden under the law than using or modifying existing buildings that house child care programs.

- Programs must assess children with disabilities upon enrollment on a case-by-case basis. Assessments must be based on individual needs, not on generalizations about a disability.

- Programs must not charge higher fees for children with disabilities than for children who are typically developing. A program can charge additional fees needed to serve one child if the cost is spread equally to all families.

- Programs cannot deny or limit children with disabilities' participation in child care activities.

- Programs cannot adopt policies that would tend to screen out children with disabilities.

Reasons for the Exclusion of Children under the ADA

A child care program might exclude a child with a disability for any of these four reasons:

Direct Threat. A program may exclude a child with a disability if inclusion poses a direct threat that cannot be eliminated by reasonable modifications. A direct threat refers to harm that could come to peers or staff member as a result of the child's disability. This is a narrow exception, because a child rarely poses a substantial risk to another child or staff members that cannot be eliminated by putting programmatic accommodations in place to prevent injury.

Fundamental Alterations. A program may exclude a child with a disability if the program would have to make fundamental alterations to the nature of services provided. This is a rare exception, too, because it would mean a child's enrollment would dramatically change how a program offers its services.

Undue Burden. A program may exclude a child with a disability if inclusion creates an undue burden for the program. The term *undue burden* means that including a child would be a significant burden or expense for the child care program. For example, if adding staff members for a child with a disability would put the program at risk financially, then this would be an undue burden. Level of burden is evaluated through the lens of overall budget and size of the organization. For instance, an undue burden for a small family child care business would be different from an undue burden for a national child care chain.

Readily Achievable. A program may exclude a child with a disability if the accommodation is not readily achievable or cannot be carried out without too much cost or difficulty. The size and budget of a program are factors in determining whether including a specific child is readily achievable under the law.

A family can file a suit with the Department of Justice if family members feel their child with a disability has been discriminated against because of the child's disability. The Department of Justice will investigate complaints if it determines there is a history of discrimination at a child care program.

The Individuals with Disabilities Education Act

The Individuals with Disabilities Education Act (IDEA) is called an entitlement law because under this law, a child who meets specific eligibility criteria is *entitled* to services. The IDEA provides early intervention and special education services to young children who qualify. The IDEA's definition of who is entitled to services is more limited than the ADA's definition. The IDEA guarantees a free and appropriate public education (FAPE) to young children with disabilities and guarantees the same access to education as children without disabilities have.

How the IDEA Defines Disability

- Young children qualify for services under a specific category in the IDEA. There are thirteen categories under which a child age three to twenty-one can qualify. They are:

  - Autism

  - Deaf-blindness

  - Deafness

  - Emotional disturbance

  - Hearing impairment

  - Intellectual disability

  - Multiple disabilities

  - Orthopedic impairment

  - Other health impairment

  - Specific learning disability

  - Speech or language impairment

  - Traumatic brain injury

  - Visual impairment (including blindness)

- Early intervention services can begin at birth.

- The IDEA serves children from birth to age twenty-one if they qualify for education services in a specific IDEA eligibility category.

- The IDEA gives an eligible child a categorical label, not a medical diagnosis. Under federal special education law, a child qualifies for services by meeting specific eligibility criteria in one of the thirteen categories. A medical diagnosis is made through a health-care process by a physician or a mental health professional. It does not guarantee special education services.

- If children are eligible for special education, they are entitled not only to special education but also to "related services" or services without which students cannot benefit from their education.

- Services for children with disabilities from birth to three years old are to occur in "natural environments." The term *natural environment* refers to the setting where a same-aged typically developing infant or toddler would be. This is usually home or a child care program. Services for three- to five-year-old children are to occur in "least restrictive environments (LREs)." This means that a child with a disability should, to the greatest extent appropriate, receive educational services with peers who don't have disabilities.

Why the IDEA Is Important to Child Care Programs

- Children three to five years old with disabilities under the IDEA should receive their services in the LRE. Child care programs are often seen as the LRE for children ages three to five years old because that is where children without disabilities are typically learning and playing together.

- Children with disabilities who are receiving services under the IDEA will have an education plan with their school district. Children from birth to three years old will have an individualized family service plan (IFSP), and children three to five years old will have an individualized education program (IEP).

- Under the IDEA, early childhood care providers can be part of the IFSP or IEP team that helps determine developmental goals for a child.

- Child care providers work with special education professionals and other specialists working with a child who has a disability to integrate IFSP or IEP goals throughout the child's routine day. This necessitates a strong partnership between families and professionals.

- All sharing of information about a child with a disability requires written permission from the parents or guardians.

Practical Application: Why Disability Law Matters to Early Educators

The overarching goal of a child care program is to help all children, with and without disabilities, reach their full learning potential within the context of the program. Disability laws are tools that help early educators support young children with disabilities in their care. For example, a speech therapist working with a child under the IDEA brings expertise to the child care setting. The ADA gives child care providers a foundation for telling all families that their program will not discriminate based on any child's special need.

Child care programs need to make reasonable accommodations for young children with disabilities under the ADA because it is a civil rights law. Here are some guidelines for achieving the goal of reasonable accommodation:

- Child care programs cannot use admissions policies that screen out or tend to screen out children with disabilities. For instance, any policy that specifies ability as a requirement for admittance could be seen as discriminating against a child with special needs.

- Programs need to modify policies, practices, or procedures that tend to screen out children with special needs unless doing so would fundamentally alter the nature of services. For example, policies against giving medications to children could be seen as a way to screen out children who have special health needs.

- Child care programs should provide auxiliary aides and services for children with disabilities unless this would create an undue burden or would fundamentally alter the nature of the program. For example, a program could provide large-print books for a child with vision issues or use a microphone for a child with hearing impairment.

- Child care programs must make physical modifications to existing facilities if they are readily achievable or can be accomplished without great expense or difficulty. Creativity can go a long way in helping a child using a wheelchair, for example, be seated with peers at the activity table or lunch table.

Child care programs can promote a child's development through important partnerships with early childhood special educators working under the IDEA. Partnerships could include the following:

- Program staff members can share general and ongoing developmental information about a child that paints a picture of the child's current developmental needs for the IFSP or IEP team. The observation and recording from child care providers is an important part of the information used in assessment.

- Providers can support a child's learning goals in their daily routines. For instance, if a child is working on speech articulation, the routine in child care might include rhyming exercises for the whole group that benefit the language development of the child with disabilities.

- Program staff members can facilitate the ongoing services provided to a child by communicating the child's progress to the special education team. Teams need to respect each other's role in the child's education.

CHAPTER 3: CREATING A SENSE OF BELONGING

Braden and Lilly are playing grocery store in the dramatic play area. Braden is checking out with his shopping list, and Lilly is ringing him up. Their laughter is contagious! Braden, who has some speech difficulties, is easily communicating to his friend that he wants to buy milk and a box of cereal. In this play area, two four-year-olds demonstrate how children have a universal language in play.

More Alike Than Different

Young children are more alike than different.

- All children need safe, nurturing, and responsive settings where they can grow and learn to their full potential.

- All children need friendships and social competencies.

- All children need to be valued for their unique abilities and personalities.

Child care providers can create an environment of acceptance for all young children, where no children are left out because they are different. In this way, each child can develop a stronger sense of self-worth and learn what it means to get along in a diverse world. This process is not without challenges. Children who do not have disabilities may have questions about a child with a disability. It is natural for young children to notice that children with disabilities are different. Children notice hair color and cultural differences. Of course they will notice a leg brace or a wheelchair!

To honor differences and highlight similarities, early childhood care providers can give brief, developmentally appropriate, and honest answers to children's questions about one another. (Confidentiality must always be observed.) The following examples show how a teacher might answer questions and comments children raise about disabilities:

"Why does Jason talk funny?" "Jason is learning to use his words, just like you are learning new things. We can help Jason by listening carefully and sharing our words with him, too."

"Will I catch what Maria has?" "Maria uses a wheelchair to help her get everywhere she needs to go. You don't need a wheelchair because you use your legs in a different way than she does. But you can both go to the park together."

"Why can't he walk like me? Is he a baby?" "You are both in the preschool room, and that's why you can be such good friends. Jonathan can't walk in exactly the same way as you, but with his braces on, he is able to walk pretty fast. His braces help him. What helps you when you are trying something new?"

"I don't want to sit by her because she makes too many noises." "Mimi is learning to tell you and me what she wants to do or play. Remember when you learned something you didn't know yet, like when you were learning to climb the slide? It takes a lot of practice. You can help Mimi by listening and showing her these pictures to see what she is asking you for. Do you want me to help you try this?"

When young children see their teachers and caregivers respond to all the children in a program with patience and parity, the children learn that while everyone has different needs, all the needs get met. This is both comforting to children and an important step toward building empathetic relationships.

Building a Caring Community

An important component of building an accepting and inclusive early childhood environment is creating a sense of belonging. Differences have less significance when all the children feel that they are integral parts of the child care program. Providers aren't ignoring differences; they are building on commonalities so friendships and relationships can thrive. One way to achieve this goal is to build a strong sense of community among children and the staff. In an inclusive child care community, all members feel they are in the right place, are welcomed, and have value.

Here are some ways to build a caring community for everyone:

Family Photos Encourage children to bring pictures of their families and share their cultural and family traditions with the group.

Children's Photos Have a place to hang photos of the children. You could include a special interest for each child. This builds a sense of belonging.

Classroom Jobs Give children jobs that help them feel invested in their setting. A jobs chart for older children helps them know that they play an important role.

Naming Songs Sing songs that name each child in the classroom.

Classroom Rules Let children choose classroom rules. This helps them have a voice in how their community functions. These rules should be simple and guided by the teacher or care provider.

Recording Daily Highlights Have children report highlights at the end of the day. Each child can report something memorable or important. You can keep these highlights in a book or post them on a board in the classroom.

Encouraging Positive Interactions Look for opportunities to talk about ways that a child supported another child, for example, through sharing or problem solving.

Family Involvement Invite families to be integral parts of the program. Encourage drop-in visits. Design family nights that have a clear function and involve the children, too. Ask for family help in creating materials, building equipment, making sensory toys, and so on.

Community Visitors Bring in members of the larger community, such as teachers, firefighters, and veterinarians, to talk about their various roles and teach children about the importance of community.

Cultural Respect Keep the child care environment alive with celebrations of the diversity of children in the program. Talk about similarities and differences. Invite people from the larger cultural community into your program to talk to the children about their cultures and customs (Croft 2007).

Young children who take ownership of their child care community will be invested in one another's outcomes. They will care about making friendships and taking care of one another. These are precursors to empathy and altruism, which we want to see in our young people as they grow older. Early childhood care providers are in a unique position to support respect and tolerance. Young children see their teachers building caring communities when they make adaptations at the lunch table for a child with a physical disability or adjust lighting for a child with sensory needs.

Policies Supporting No Expulsion

A program philosophy supporting no expulsions is a key strategy for teaching all children that everyone belongs. Here are some facts to consider:

- Child care program expulsion is often the outcome for challenging behaviors in young children.

- Preschool expulsion is three times higher than expulsion rates for kindergarten through grade twelve (Gilliam 2008).

- Expulsion has not been shown to be effective at reducing future behavioral issues in young children.

- A 2014 policy statement from the US Department of Health and Human Services and the US Department of Education highlights the need for attention in the early childhood field to "prevent, severely limit, and work toward eventually eliminating expulsion and suspension . . . of young children" (US DHHS and US DOE 2014, 1).

- The American Academy of Pediatrics recommends that "children . . . at risk for expulsion should be assessed for developmental, behavioral, and medical problems to identify underlying concerns that might be targeted through intervention services" (Gilliam 2008, 7).

All young children are learning how to interact in a complicated social world with little experience. A child with a disability may have even more limited skills for navigating the social scene of child care than a child without a disability. When adults teach all children, with and without disabilities, new and more appropriate behaviors to replace challenging behaviors, we show children that it's important that everyone knows how to get along.

To prevent expulsion, you can take several proactive steps. Provide clear expectations and behavior guidelines in your family handbook. Connect with local supports that provide you with tools. Observe and document. Stay connected with families. Develop an intervention plan with the staff and families.

Provide Clear Expectations and Behavior Guidelines in Your Family Handbook

- Develop a clear plan for steps that will be taken when extreme behavior challenges occur.

- Provide these guidelines to all parents and guardians upon enrollment.

- Make it a policy to refrain from expelling or suspending children, and spell out the ways in which you as a care provider will seek support.

- Make it clear how you expect families to seek assistance and answers through early childhood screening or a mental health referral.

Connect with Local Supports That Provide You with Tools

- Find other providers in your area with whom you can meet regularly or connect on the phone. Build a positive support network in your area.

- Enroll in trainings, especially those that focus on guidance strategies, mental health, and social-emotional development.

- Know the contact information of school districts, local hospitals, and assessment and evaluation providers in the community.

Observe and Document

- Upon each child's enrollment in the program, start taking notes about the day-to-day behaviors you observe. These notes will help you track a child's social-emotional development and tune in to any behavior changes or challenges that may arise.

- For a child with behavior challenges, keep a running record of what engages the child when calm, peers with whom the child has positive interactions, and information the family shares about the child's home routine and sleep pattern. This information will help guide your behavioral strategies with the child.

Stay Connected with Families

- If you have concerns about a child's development or about a pattern of challenging behavior, it is critical to talk with parents or guardians daily.

- Building a relationship of trust with the child and the family is critical when working with a child who exhibits challenges.

- Build a relationship of trust by listening to their concerns and by providing tips for home, primarily to help them get through the tough times and assure them that they are not alone.

Develop an Intervention Plan with Staff Members and Families

- When there are recurring behavior challenges, it is vital to develop a written plan. This plan creates consistency and follow-through while bridging home life and child care.

- Meet with all of the caregivers in a child's life and discuss possible interventions as responses to the child's behavior. For instance, if transitions are difficult, you may decide that an individual picture schedule for the daily routine will help the child move from activity to activity. Such interventions can increase the odds of success as you try to change behavior patterns.

(Center for Inclusive Child Care 2014. Used with permission.)

CHAPTER 4: TYPICAL AND ATYPICAL DEVELOPMENT

Evelyn is a three-year-old who has been attending Sunny Days Child Care for two months. Her teacher has noticed that she still plays alone much of the time rather than joining in with peers. She seems to prefer to stay in the same play routine and engage in repetitive activity. Looking over her written observations since Evelyn was enrolled, the teacher sees a pattern of disengagement and lack of social skills development. She makes a note to talk to Evelyn's family about her concerns.

Defining Typical and Atypical Development

Children's development is an ongoing process of growth, change, and constancy from prebirth to adolescence across six primary domains. These developmental domains are as follows:

Cognitive Development. Cognitive development is the ability to learn and solve problems. For example, Jason, who is four years old, goes to the peace table with his friend Jessica to solve a dispute over whose turn it is to use the art easel. They talk it over by passing a teddy bear back and forth until they reach an agreement they both like.

Social-Emotional Development. Social-emotional development is the ability to interact with others and control one's emotions and impulses. For instance, two-year-old Marisol is content to play by herself but is also beginning to be interested in playing next to peers. She isn't yet ready to play *with* a friend, but she likes being near others while they all play with their own toys.

Speech and Language Development. Speech and language development is the ability to understand and use language. For example, four-month-old Sasha coos loudly at her primary caregiver. As she receives smiles in exchange for the sounds, she vocalizes even more.

Fine-Motor Skill Development. Fine-motor skill development is the ability to use small muscles, specifically in the hands and fingers. For instance, three-year-old Phillippe uses the Duplo blocks to build a tower that he will knock down with the race car.

Gross-Motor Skill Development. Gross-motor skill development is the ability to use large muscles for movement and other activities. For example, five-year-old Malcolm goes up and down the slide over and over again during outside play.

Adaptive Skill Development. Adaptive skill development includes self-care and daily living skills. For instance, the children in the three-year-old classroom wash their hands before snack by standing in a line and taking turns at the sink. One person gets the job of holding the soap dispenser and squirting it into each child's hand.

(Adapted from "Developmental Delay" tip sheet, Center for Inclusive Child Care 2015.)

Young children change month by month in each of these six developmental domains. Most children will develop typically, within a range of expectations at each age and stage of development.

Typical Development

Typical development is regarded as what peers of the same age are accomplishing during an expected time period or stage. Early childhood development specialists Eileen Allen and Glynnis Cowdery refer to typical development as the pathway whereby children acquire a range of complex skills through growth and change (Allen and Cowdery 2012). For instance, typical gross-motor skill development in a six-month-old would include rolling over in both directions and beginning to sit up alone.

The development of a particular skill within a developmental domain is known as a developmental milestone:

- Developmental milestones can be seen as checkpoints at various ages and stages. These checkpoints are based on theories of child development that help adults track children's growth.

- Milestones are sets of functional skills or age-specific tasks based on what most children at a given age are doing at that age and stage.

- We use developmental milestones as measurements to gauge children's progress so we can adapt to their specific learning needs and provide therapeutic interventions if progress is delayed.

- Mastery of milestones can be influenced by internal stressors such as poor nutrition, disability, low birth weight, and lack of sleep.

- Mastery of milestones can also be influenced by external stressors such as neglect, poverty, inconsistent care, and culture.

- When we see that milestones are not being mastered, we turn our attention to atypical development.

Atypical Development

Atypical development deviates from what is typical for a child at a given age and stage. For example, we expect to see a child walk around twelve months of age. If the child is not

walking at this age and doesn't display ongoing motor development such as pulling up and crawling, the child would be considered atypically developing in gross-motor skills. Atypical development can mean either delayed or accelerated development. Atypical development is a lens through which we can recognize young children who may have different characteristics in some areas but who are similar to other children in their potential for growth (Allen and Cowdery 2012).

Children do grow at different rates, so it is important for early childhood professionals to observe and record development of each child across milestones in order to be aware of children's progress. Following are some key concepts to keep in mind:

- We expect variations in development among young children.

- While we can predict certain sequences of development because of milestones, we also know that all children are unique, with individual characteristics.

- We become concerned when development does not continue in a predictable manner.

- It is not unusual for a child to be progressing typically and then slow down in one skill area while working on mastery of another. For example, a child may be progressing rapidly in speech and language skills, but the child's behavior may become unpredictable during the process of learning new ways to communicate with others and problem solve.

Red Flags for Developmental Delays: Implications for Child Care

Red flags in development are behaviors that should warn you, as a care provider, to stop, look, and think. In other words, take some time to consider whether a child's developmental trajectory is consistent with typical child development.

Look for patterns or clusters of a behavior. Does a toddler have difficulty with all fine-motor activities or just with using a spoon? Is there a physical delay, or does the child have limited experience with self-feeding?

Observe a child in a variety of situations. A two-year-old may not use many words in the art area, but when you observe the child in dramatic play, you hear much more expressive language. Try to get a complete picture of the child's development across activities.

Compare the child's current behavior to a norm of six months younger and six months older. Developmental milestones have ranges, because all children develop at their own rate.

Note how much the child has grown in the past three to six months; has the child progressed? Keep track of a child's progress over time to determine mastery of skills. If an eighteen-month-old is using five or six words, and three months later is still using only those same words, that is a red flag for developmental concern.

Know the typical patterns of child growth and development. Be familiar with typical child development. Web pages such as the Centers for Disease Control and Prevention's "Learn the Signs. Act Early." (www.cdc.gov/ncbddd/actearly/index.html) are good sources for up-to-date developmental information.

Keep in mind the factors that may be influencing development. A child may have been developing on track, and then slows or even regresses. For instance, a three-year-old may be toilet trained but begin to have accidents again. Consider other factors in a child's life, such as changes in home life, trauma or stress, and illness, which can affect development. Having a strong relationship with the child's family is important when considering what might be influencing a child's development.

If a child is not mastering a milestone and there are other red flags as well, talking to the family about a referral to early intervention is appropriate practice. Red flags point us to potential developmental gaps and give us information we need to make appropriate referrals to early intervention services and also to make accommodations in our classrooms.

Observation and Assessment

It is a critical role of the early childhood educator to use ongoing observation and assessment tools to track children's development. Keep these ideas in mind as you observe and assess the children in your care:

- If a teacher observes red flags in a child's development, this could indicate a delay in one of the developmental domains.

- A developmental delay means a child is not reaching particular developmental milestones at the expected time.

- Allen and Cowdery explain delay as "when a child is performing like a child of a much younger age who is typically developing" (2012, 90).

- It is important to note that all children continue to grow and develop, even with disabilities; it is the rate of growth and the mastery of milestones that pose the developmental differences.

- A developmental delay may be major or minor; with intervention, many delays are overcome.

- Working closely with the family and other professionals (with family consent) can ensure that everyone is working for the same developmental outcomes for the young child.

Practical Application: Supporting the Development of Children with Atypical Needs

An effective intervention for a child with a special need will usually be a good learning practice for all children. As teachers support children with atypical developmental needs, here are a few ways to ensure you are promoting positive outcomes for everyone:

Keep ongoing developmental records on all children. When you are documenting, use specific, objective, and nonjudgmental developmental language. Having factual information on hand will help when you need to share developmental concerns with a family.

Be knowledgeable about your local early intervention referral contacts. When you talk to a family about red flags in their child's development, give them information so they can call to set up a screening or evaluation. You may even want to offer to make the call with them as a support.

Be aware that you may be the first person to bring up a developmental concern to a family. Family members may have suspected a delay and be relieved to have another person validate their concerns, or they may be resistant to the information you share. Either way, the family needs to know that you are supporting them and that you will continue to provide developmentally appropriate practices for their child.

Adapt lesson planning and activities to meet each child's individual needs. Consider the overall goal of any activity. For instance, if the children are creating a cooperative fingerpainting (the activity) in order to help them learn friendship skills (the goal), you can provide multiple ways for each child to play a role in making the painting. A child may fingerpaint differently—with gloves or with a cotton swab—but still be painting together with peers. You can help all children meet the goal of the activity by individualizing it to the child's needs.

Build mutually respectful relationships with families and other professionals. Everyone works together to meet the needs of a child. Families are the child's first teachers; they are a valuable resource for making adaptations. Therapists who may be working with the child can help generalize specific goals into everyday child care activities. (Confidentiality is the law, so parents or guardians need to give written consent for professionals to share information with others.)

What works for a child with a disability is usually useful to the whole classroom. If a child with autism reacts to sensory input, having a classroom that's not overloaded with sensory stimuli can help all the children be less aroused by the environment. If a child with speech difficulties benefits from rhyming, all the children can learn from using rhymes. If your setting is less cluttered so a wheelchair can be maneuvered, this means that all children are less likely to trip over a loose rug or trikes in the hallway.

Parents as Partners

The earlier an intervention can be started, the better the outcomes for a child will be. Including parents, guardians, and other family members as partners when enrolling a child with atypical needs is a key step to successful inclusion. Gather as much information as possible so your setting will be welcoming and will provide a sense of safety to the child and the family. Families of children with disabilities and families of children who are typically developing want similar things for their children: protection, security, friends, and belonging. The following box outlines some specific areas to consider when enrolling a child with a disability. Ask the family these questions to help you be successful in including their child:

For my setting, what accommodations would you recommend that are specific to your child's needs?

What is your child's medical history?

What past medical concerns could affect activities in child care? If your child has had a recent surgery, are there restrictions on play?

What medications does your child need to be successful here?

If your child has diabetes, how often does glucose testing need to be done? Who will administer insulin?

What information about your child and your family do you want shared with the staff? How do we protect your child's confidentiality while also ensuring safety?

How does your child interact with others?

Does your child who is nonverbal have a special way to communicate with others? Can we teach this to the other children?

Does your child need prompts to enter play with peers? Does your child favor solitary or cooperative play? What are your child's favorite activities?

Does your child prefer some time to warm up upon arrival in the morning, or is your child ready to play right away?

Does your child with sensory issues prefer not to be hugged by everyone upon arrival?

How does your child eat? Will we need any special equipment?

Does your child have any allergies? What is the medical plan for allergic reactions?

What are your child's positioning needs?

If your child has gross-motor delays, will we need specialized equipment to facilitate mobility and physical, developmental, and social interaction? What are the goals of the equipment for your child?

What works well at home?

Can your child signal discomfort or a need to change positions?

What are your child's toileting needs?

Are there other specialists or therapists from whom we could seek information or with whom we could partner?

With your written consent, what other professionals could share therapy approaches or strategies with the child care staff to ensure consistency of approaches and goals?

Would other specialists be willing to come in to the child care center and train staff members to support your child's special need?

If your child has an IFSP or IEP, do you want your child care provider to be involved with the special education team? What would be the role of the child care provider?

CHAPTER 5: ANXIETY DISORDER

Annika, who is three, cries inconsolably when her mom drops her off at child care. It can take more than ten minutes for her to settle herself so she can join her friends in free play. Her teacher knows that Annika has experienced trauma in her young life, which keeps her on high alert. Her teacher makes sure to greet Annika the same way each morning, with a stuffed bear that she loves to hold until she is ready to play.

Defining Anxiety Disorder

Anxiety is a common emotion for both children and adults. Every child experiences worry and anxiousness from time to time, whether it is from changes at home, like a new baby sibling, or beginning a new child care program. Even small changes in routines, like going on a field trip or having a substitute teacher, can provoke anxiety.

An anxiety disorder is different from typical feelings of anxiousness in a young child. Anxiety disorders are characterized by overwhelming feelings of anxiousness, fearfulness, or a loss of control that interfere with relationships, interactions, and learning (MACMH 2016). Anxiety disorder is the most common mental health disorder in children.

There are several types of anxiety disorders. The Anxiety and Depression Association of America lists the following kinds of anxiety disorders that may be diagnosed in children and adolescents:

- Generalized anxiety disorder (GAD)
- Separation anxiety disorder
- Obsessive-compulsive disorder (OCD)
- Panic disorder
- Post-traumatic stress disorder (PTSD)
- Selective mutism
- Social anxiety disorder
- Specific phobias

Anxiety disorders are more common in older children and adolescents than in preschoolers. Anxiety disorders should be diagnosed by a mental health professional through a comprehensive psychiatric and health evaluation. Early intervention is important to help young children develop coping skills for handling anxious situations and feelings.

Characteristics of Children with Anxiety Disorder: Implications for Child Care

Helping children feel safe and secure in a consistent care setting is an important goal for early educators. It is important to know the difference between normal and extreme anxiety. For example, a child experiencing the normal separation anxiety of a two-year-old is different from a child who breaks a shoelace and cannot be calmed. Following are some key concepts to consider:

- All children will experience anxiousness at times.

- It is common for toddlers to cling to their primary caregiver when someone strange is near and to have separation anxiety when their primary caregiver leaves.

- Most children outgrow typical anxiety by age three, as they become more autonomous.

- Mild stressors such as storms, loud noises, the dark, and strangers commonly trigger anxiousness in children from one to five years old.

- The difference between normal anxiety and anxiety disorder is the duration and intensity of the child's feelings and reactions.

- A child with an anxiety disorder will not be calmed as easily with verbal reassurances as will a child who feels normal anxiety.

- A child who experiences excessive worry and fearfulness needs professional intervention along with the support of responsive and nurturing caregiving.

- For a child with anxiety disorder who may have experienced trauma and neglect or who cannot regulate out-of-control feelings, the child care environment can be a tool to support feelings of safety and security.

Generalized Anxiety Disorder

Children with GAD have great difficulty controlling their worries or fears. They may worry about something happening to them or their families, their pets, their classrooms, or almost anything else. This persistent worry keeps them from engaging in learning activities and play that they need in order to develop their cognitive and social-emotional skills. Providers can use the following strategies to support children with GAD in the child care setting:

- Minimize schedule changes and transitions as much as possible.

- Provide opportunities for children to express emotions. Keep feelings charts or wheels available so children can tell you when they are feeling worried.

- When children are anxious, stay calm and help them talk through the anxiousness.

- Help children with strategies to regulate the anxiety they have expressed. For instance, use relaxation techniques like deep breathing. Practice these strategies together so they become familiar and easy to remember.

- Use therapeutic teacher talk to reassure children that they are safe by saying, "You are safe here," or, "I'll be here tomorrow."

Separation Anxiety Disorder

Separation anxiety disorder means a child may be extremely upset to be away from a parent or a primary caregiver and worry that some harm will come to them (ADAA 2015). This is different from a toddler with separation anxiety who is settled with soothing by his caregiver or by getting engaged in play.

An early childhood setting can offer support to a child with separation anxiety by using these strategies:

- Maintain consistent routines with consistent staff members to support regulation.

- Build a sense of security and safety with physical boundaries, such as by using shelves to separate activity areas.

- Use visual supports to build regulation, such as posted rules or a daily picture schedule. These reinforce consistency and routine for children.

These are the most common anxiety disorders seen in young children, but other types of anxiety disorders may be diagnosed in children and adolescents, too. Parents and mental health professionals working with the child will be essential resources for specific environmental supports for the child. The strategies offered in this chapter help all children feel safe and secure, but they are particularly helpful for those children with anxiousness and anxiety issues.

Red Flags for Anxiety Disorder

A child with an anxiety disorder may not have a diagnosis upon enrollment in an early childhood program. That's why it is important for adults to know how to distinguish between typical anxiety in a young child and the characteristics of a mental health disorder. Ongoing observation and recording will establish a developmental picture of the child's behaviors, which will be valuable in a formal assessment. Red flags for a mental health disorder in a young child can be subtle to an observer, so documentation needs to be consistent,

ongoing, and across various times of day and across various activities. Be aware of the following facts during your ongoing observations:

- Observations can reveal a pattern that indicates atypical behaviors in a child.

- It can be difficult to know what young children are experiencing because of their limited language development and cognitive ability.

- Children may not be able to express what is happening when they are afraid or anxious.

- Anxiety disorders are more commonly diagnosed in children after age six (Child Mind Institute 2015).

Referral to an early intervention professional or a mental health professional is important if any of the following red flags are observed in a young child:

- Difficulty with transitions

- Unexpected fearfulness

- Challenging behaviors

- Unexplained and frequent crying

- Withdrawing or isolating behaviors

- Jumpiness or nervousness at typical sounds or changes in the environment

- Excessive worry

- Frequent thoughts of dread

- Frequent physical symptoms like stomachaches and headaches

- Need for constant reassurances

- Trouble making friends or having no friends

- Difficulty sleeping

> These red flags can also be signs of a child who is experiencing trauma or has another type of developmental disability, such as autism spectrum disorder. Helping the family by making a referral to early intervention will start the process for finding the right diagnosis for a young child.

Practical Application: Strategies for Including Children with Anxiety Disorder

Including a child with an anxiety disorder involves setting up the environment in a predictable and consistent way. This has the benefit of helping all young children feel safe and secure as they develop socially and emotionally. Here are some strategies for creating predictability and consistency:

Use a visual picture schedule. Referring throughout the day to scheduled activities helps build regulatory skills in children. Each time you say, "Look at the wall; it's time for snack now," it shows young children that there is a routine that stays the same each day. This is especially important for a child who struggles with anxiety.

Keep a regular schedule and regular routines. As much as possible, keep routines the same. Keep the same activities in the same area, and keep the same toys in the same containers. Classroom routines help children feel boundaries and limits. Routines build a sense of security.

Plan ahead for transitions and changes. Let children know when a change will happen. With children who are anxious, use tools they may help them make the change more smoothly, such as having them hold their favorite sensory objects. If you've worked on a cue for changes, practice the cue as well. This might be as simple as a hand on the child's shoulder.

Practice relaxation techniques. Help children recognize when they are becoming anxious and practice ways to regulate themselves, such as relaxation techniques. Relaxation techniques might include deep breathing or reframing negative thoughts. Work with other professionals who serve a child with anxiety to make sure the techniques are consistent and useful.

Watch for sensory overload. Tune in to the sounds, sights, and smells of your program. Where could you adapt the environment to make it calmer? Watch for cues that a child is becoming overstimulated, which can increase anxiousness.

Don't dismiss a fear. Brushing off a fear can make a child feel rejected or insecure. Overattention to a fear can make it bigger than it is. Keep a balance for the child that validates the child's feelings without giving strength to the fear.

Build a sense of safety and security. All children benefit when they feel emotionally secure. Security supports children's attachment, ongoing exploration, and creativity. A chaotic environment will promote feelings of insecurity.

Allow transitional objects. If a child feels more secure with a blanket from home, allow the object in your setting. Early educators can make rules for how transitional objects are used, whether that means keeping it in the child's cubby where it can be visited anytime or holding it at naptime only.

Know a child's interests and build activities around them. Activities that extend and expand a child's interest areas will help the child stay engaged and actively learning longer.

Work closely with families and with other professionals. If a child has a diagnosis of anxiety disorder, ask the parents or guardians for permission to talk to the mental health professionals working with their child. Strategies for calming used in therapy may also be embedded in the child care setting.

Anxiety disorder is managed better the earlier it is diagnosed. Without intervention, a child may experience difficulties with social competence, academics, and self-esteem. The early childhood program is a place where a child with anxiety disorder can make friends and learn new skills—if it is set up for the child's success.

CHAPTER 6: ATTENTION DEFICIT/ HYPERACTIVITY DISORDER

Stephan, who is five years old, has been an active child ever since he began walking and talking. He is very interested in the world around him and in what everyone is doing. Sometimes he cannot stay engaged in an activity for as long as his friends, so he tends to move around his classroom a lot during free-play time or choice time. His teacher helps him by narrowing his choices down to two or three. She says she appreciates him because he always has new ideas for play. It is hard for him when something out of the ordinary is going on in the room, such as a visitor or a celebration.

Defining Attention Deficit/Hyperactivity Disorder

According to the Centers for Disease Control and Prevention (CDC), attention deficit/hyperactivity disorder (ADHD) is neurological condition that may occur as commonly as in one of every ten children. Researchers do not know the cause of ADHD, though studies suggest genetics may play a role. Other studies link ADHD to some neurotoxins, such as lead and tobacco smoke. Parenting style does not cause ADHD, though it does influence the behaviors of a child with the disability.

While the cause of ADHD is yet unknown, its impact on young children's ability to learn, gain social competencies, and regulate themselves is recognized. Many children at different ages will struggle with attention, activity level, and regulatory skills as part of their ongoing physical, emotional, and cognitive development. Children with ADHD will have difficulty managing their behavior in a way that is appropriate for their age level and developmental stage.

A diagnosis should be made by a neurologist, pediatrician, or mental health professional to rule out other disabilities that might look like ADHD. There is no single test for diagnosing a child with ADHD, but a comprehensive evaluation will include family history, written observations from the child care provider and others who know the child, behavior rating scales, intelligence testing, and a neurological and medical exam to rule out other issues.

The medical diagnosis specifies one of three presentations for ADHD:

- Predominantly inattentive presentation: This presentation has mainly inattentive symptoms with few or no hyperactive symptoms.

- Predominantly hyperactive/impulsive presentation: This presentation has mainly hyperactive and impulsive symptoms with few or no inattentive symptoms.

- Combined presentation: This presentation has symptoms of both inattention and hyperactivity.

Early intervention is crucial for helping young children learn skills to cope with some of the aspects of ADHD. They can receive negative attention from both adults and peers for behaviors that are often part of ADHD. This negative attention can result in low self-worth, which compounds behavioral issues. Setting a child up for success in the early childhood program can help a child develop lifelong skills for academic learning and for developing social relationships.

Characteristics of Children with Attention Deficit/ Hyperactivity Disorder: Implications for Child Care

An attention disorder is a problem affecting all areas of children's interactions with their environments. Children experiencing ADHD commonly have difficulty in the following broad areas:

- Inattention and distractibility

- Hyperactivity

- Impulsivity

Inattention, hyperactivity, and impulsivity are common behaviors in all young children, particularly preschoolers who are just beginning to master regulatory skills in their social-emotional development. A child with ADHD will engage in these behaviors more frequently and for longer periods of time than a peer without ADHD will.

Several characteristics of children with ADHD can present challenges in the child care setting:

Inattention and Distractibility Children who have inattention and distractibility may have a hard time staying in an activity area for very long or may move from area to area without ever engaging. They may disrupt others who are playing by interrupting their games or by seeking attention with challenging behaviors. Circle time can be difficult for children who are distractible unless they have tools to help them tune in for group time, such as a fidget to hold or a carpet square to sit on.

Hyperactivity Children who have hyperactive behaviors are moving all the time. It can be difficult to do story time if a child with ADHD can't sit for long and is up and down a lot. A child with hyperactivity can influence actions in other children at times, such as by chasing other children. Hyperactivity differs from the typical activity level that is part of a child's temperament. A child may be on the high end of activity as a part of temperament but still not be hyperactive. Children with ADHD will be busier for longer periods of time and will be less able to control their activity levels than peers will.

Impulsivity A child with low impulse control has a hard time pausing between a thought and an action. All children need to learn to regulate impulses as part of their development, but a child with high impulsivity is a child who acts first and thinks later. If a friend accidently knocks over the child's block tower, the child may hit a friend on the head with a block instead of saying, "That makes me so mad at you!" A child with high impulsivity needs strategies from adults in order to learn how to stop and wait before acting.

Red Flags for Attention Deficit/Hyperactivity Disorder

Impulsivity, inattention, and high activity level are all traits that each child has to some degree. A child with ADHD will experience these traits with more intensity than a child who does not have ADHD. Observing children's behaviors over a period of time and across activities in child care will help a teacher prepare to talk to families about red flags for developmental concerns. Here are some red flags for families and teachers to be aware of:

- Cannot engage for periods of time in age-appropriate activities

- Moves or fidgets more than peers

- Talks a lot and interrupts others who are talking

- Daydreams instead of paying attention

- Doesn't complete tasks or activities without much adult prompting

- Has difficulty getting along with peers

- Has difficulty following directions

- Has difficulty organizing self and tasks

- Has trouble waiting for turn

All of these are common occasional behaviors in preschoolers and young children. The frequency, intensity, and duration of the behaviors at both home and child care are factors in determining whether children are behaving typically for their age or seem to be having developmental issues that warrant evaluation. If evaluation is necessary, it is important to help families with referrals to early intervention or medical specialists.

Practical Application: Strategies for Including Children with Attention Deficit/Hyperactivity Disorder

A child with ADHD can be more successful if an early childhood setting is consistent, has clear boundaries, is structured, and offers opportunities for choices. The following are some specific strategies for including children with inattention, impulsivity, and hyperactivity:

Inattention and Distractibility

- Make sure your interest areas matter to the children. Ask them for ideas.

- Give choices—but not too many choices, which might overwhelm a child.

- Put materials out as an activity progresses rather than putting everything out at once. Too many materials can be distracting and confusing.

- Let children who have trouble paying attention sit close to an adult during circle time or story time. Give directions one step at a time.

- Talk less and act more. Children with ADHD may not listen for long, so be concise when giving directions or feedback.

- Help children be organized. Label items in the program so children know where everything goes when it is time to choose a play activity or to clean up. Label backpacks and other personal items so children can easily spot what they need to gather to go outside or to go home for the day.

Impulsivity

- Give children immediate feedback and consequences. Children with ADHD may forget a behavior if the reinforcement comes long after the action. Use positive incentives more than negative consequences.

- Provide a quiet space for children to calm themselves and get away from sensory overload.

- Teach children how to recognize and name their feelings. This helps children avoid aggression as their first impulse. Have a classroom rich in emotional literacy. Encourage children when they use words to describe big feelings.

- Use visual timers, such as Time Timers, to help children be aware of the beginning and end of activities and to support transitions.

- Give children fidgets to hold during difficult times, such as wait times.

- Use visual supports such as picture symbols to represent the steps of an activity. For instance, post pictures of the steps for hand washing.

- Make clear boundaries. Use carpet squares for children to sit on. Set the table with place mats so children know where their space is. Use shelving and other equipment to make physical boundaries.

Hyperactivity

- Engage a child's senses with diverse sensory experiences. Offer opportunities to spend longer amounts of time in dramatic play or at the water table.

- Allow plenty of time for gross-motor play that uses balance and proprioception (body awareness). Marching, swinging, and outdoor playtime help children get input to their large muscles and joints and stimulate their sense of balance and body awareness.

- Have a fidget basket always available to children when they need to keep their hands busy or when they simply need movement. Keep a selection of fidgets that provide different sensory input, such as Koosh balls, Slinkies, Tangles, and glitter wands. Different types of fidgets will appeal to different children depending on their sensory preferences for size, texture, motion, and so on.

- Be organized and have materials ready before an activity begins in order to avoid making children wait.

- Teach a child relaxation techniques. For example, when you are moving from a fast-paced activity to a quieter one, ask, "How fast is your engine running? How can you slow it down?"

- Give children opportunities to do resistive work like pushing or pulling a basket of blocks, "holding up" the wall by pressing on it, washing the tables, and so on. This can be calming to a child's senses.

- Incorporate calming activities, like blowing bubbles, into the day.

> The physical environment plays a critical role in the success of a child with ADHD. The emotional environment is important as well, so encourage children with ADHD as they are completing a task or paying attention. Appreciate that characteristics common to children with ADHD are positive attributes, too, and can serve children as they grow and learn to be independent, creative, and fun to be around.

CHAPTER 7: AUTISM SPECTRUM DISORDER

Timothy, who has autism, is fascinated by airplanes. He carries a toy airplane in his pocket at all times. He loves books about aircraft and wants to land his plane on the runway he builds in the Lego area. His teacher makes a buddy bucket containing a puzzle of an airplane and other small manipulatives that fly, like birds and pterodactyls. She pairs Jamie and Timothy as play partners to encourage social interaction and friendship skills.

Defining Autism Spectrum Disorder

Autism spectrum disorder (ASD) is a neurological disorder that interferes with a child's ability to communicate and interact with others. It is considered a spectrum disorder because there is a wide range in the impact of the disability on each child in terms of symptoms, skills, and severity. Given the current rate of diagnosis, it is likely that at some point most early educators will enroll a child with autism in their program. So, it is important to understand ASD, including ways to make general adaptations to your environment and programming for successful inclusion.

Here are some facts about ASD:

- In its 2016 study, the Centers for Disease Control and Prevention reports ASD occurs in one in sixty-eight children.

- In 2005, the prevalence of autism was 1 in 166. That means the rate of occurrence has changed significantly over ten years.

- There is no single medical test to diagnose autism. Specialists use a variety of tools to determine an autism diagnosis under the *Diagnostic and Statistical Manual of Mental Disorders, Fifth Edition (DSM-5)*.

- ASD occurs in every racial and ethnic group and across all socioeconomic levels.

- Boys are identified with autism at a rate four times higher than that of girls.

- Families who have one child with autism have a greater risk of having another child with autism.

- Children who have older parents have a greater risk of autism. Risk increases as women age past thirty (with greater risk after age forty) and as men age past forty.

- Autism is a lifelong developmental disability.

- The causes of autism are unknown.

At this time there is no cure for autism spectrum disorder, according to leading health organizations such as the CDC. However, early interventions, including social-emotional support, speech and language therapy, and other behavioral interventions, have significant developmental impact on young children with autism. The earlier a child receives a diagnosis, the more positive are the outcomes.

Characteristics of Children with ASD: Implications for Child Care

Since ASD is a spectrum disorder, its impact on development for each child is unique. Children with autism spectrum disorder may experience a range of impacts on their development in the following areas:

Problems in Communication and Social Interaction Children with autism may not speak, may have very few words, or may only repeat words they hear. Children with autism may have strong vocabulary and high memorization but may lack responsive language skills. They may have problems understanding facial expressions of peers or typical play behaviors.

Behaviors or Interests That Are Rigid and Repetitive Children with autism might engage in the same behavior, such as spinning in circles or playing with only one toy, over and over again. They may show a preference for an activity that is very hard to transition from.

Red Flags for Autism Spectrum Disorder

Autism can be identified early in a child's life through screening and evaluation by medical professionals and early childhood intervention specialists. Some red flags for autism can be observed in the first two years of life:

- Families often report suspecting a developmental issue in their young child with autism before a diagnosis has been made.

- It is important for the early childhood care provider to observe and record development for all children in a program, because these notes can be included in the informal assessment process when information is shared with families.

- If red flags are identified, a referral should be made to local early intervention, or the notes should be used in the physician visit.

Not all children with ASD will have all the same red flags for early developmental concerns. However, some general red flags follow:

In Social Interactions

- Overattachment to certain objects
- No smiling or happy expressions by six months of age
- Rigidity in making changes; great difficulty with transitions
- Resistance to cuddling or physical attention
- Difficulty with imitation skills
- Difficulty with reciprocal social interaction
- Difficulty with make-believe or dramatic play
- Inability to play with peers
- Preference for being alone, playing in solitary play
- Lack of eye contact and facial expression
- Difficulty expressing needs and feelings
- Difficulty making and keeping friends
- Loss of social skills at any age

In Behavior Patterns

- No gesturing or pointing by fourteen months of age
- Uneven gross- and fine-motor skills; problems with coordination
- Unresponsiveness to verbal cues
- Little or no eye contact
- Use of repetitive movements like flapping or rocking
- Insistence on sameness; resistance to change in routine
- Noticeable physical overactivity or underactivity
- Displays of extreme distress for no apparent reason
- Fixation on an object
- Sensitivity to light, noise, smell, or textures

In Speech and Communication

- No babbling or cooing by twelve months of age

- Loss of previously acquired language at any age

- Inappropriate laughing and giggling

- Use of gestures or pointing without using any words that are age-appropriate

- Appearance of not hearing at times

- Echolalia (repeating words or phrases in place of typical language); unusual use of speech

- Abnormalities in nonverbal communication, as in eye contact, facial expressions, body postures, or gestures to initiate social interaction

- Abnormalities in production of speech, as in volume, pitch, or rhythm

- Abnormalities in sound of speech, like monotone, high pitch, or odd inflections

(Adapted from Center for Inclusive Child Care 2011.)

Practical Application: Strategies for Including Children with ASD

What we know about young children with autism can help us as we plan environmental adaptions for successful inclusion. Here are a few ways to meet specific needs:

Children with autism are highly visual learners. This means that using visual supports, such as picture schedules, cue cards, photos with words, feelings wheels, and other picture tools, will facilitate communication and learning. A choice board is another tool that gives children a visual representation of options they have for activities, food, and other daily experiences.

Change and transitions can be challenging for children with autism. For some children with autism, doing the same task over and over is a common behavior. A child may perseverate, or repeat a task insistently. This can cause a child to lose out on social time with peers because play is solitary; in addition, a child with autism may react strongly when the preferred behavior is interrupted.

Children with autism like routines and predictability. Routines and predictability are important for all young children. Routines help children learn regulatory skills and also help children feel secure. Children with ASD need a sense of predictability in order to engage and connect to the world around them. This can be achieved with group and individual picture schedules, a stable classroom environment, and consistent staffing.

Children with autism tend to be literal rather than abstract learners and communicators. To communicate effectively with a child who has autism, use concrete language as much as possible. Use visual supports for teaching concepts. Children with autism may struggle with idioms. For example, *it's raining cats and dogs* may be confusing to a child with autism when there are no animals in the sky.

Children with autism can have difficulty making friends. Social competencies may be hard for a child with autism, especially if the child has language difficulties or problems understanding facial expressions and abstract feelings. If the child prefers solitary and repetitive play, it can be hard for other children to join in. Play skills may be an area in which children with ASD need active support from an adult, to practice play and words for entering play.

Adaptations for children with ASD will often be strategies that support learning for all the children in your program. In general, an organized and consistent program that incorporates visual supports works well for children who have autism. If a child is working with specialists such as speech therapists, they may have specific strategies for building skills that can be embedded in the child's daily routine at child care.

The following are strategies for adaptation across the three main areas of impact that autism can have on a child:

Social Interaction

- Build on a child's interests. If a child fixates on airplanes, extend and expand activities to include airports, transportation, or other things that fly.

- Create buddy buckets as a way to help a child increase social interaction. Pair a child who has autism with a peer who has strong social skills, and give them a bucket filled with items from the main interest area of the child who has ASD.

- Give preschoolers with autism words for entering play with others, such as *I would like to be a firefighter* for a group playing firehouse in dramatic play.

- Give a child a preferred play item, such as a race car to enter a group playing cars.

- Plan carefully for transitions, whether for changing activities or for going to a different classroom. Talk ahead of time about a change in the schedule, such as a field trip.

- To prepare a child for a transition, use cues like a visual schedule showing the coming change or a visual cue card for when an activity is ending.

- Use repetition to teach social skills. Children with autism may need to practice play skills or phrases that help them interact.

- For an older preschooler, use dramatic play or role play to practice taking another person's perspective. Practice responses to another child crying or telling a joke.

- Use feelings wheels and cubes, emotions mirrors, feelings posters, and books to teach preschoolers with autism about their own feelings and what feelings look like on peers.

- Occasionally provide opportunities for quiet time or individual activities. Watch for over-scheduling with peers.

Behavior Patterns

- Evaluate your sensory environment. Be aware of what sensory stimulation tends to arouse a child with autism, so you can remove it or lessen its impact.

- Keep loud sounds to a minimum where possible; prepare a child with autism for fire drills or other emergency drills.

- Have a pair of earphones for a child who sometimes needs to muffle sound. Use area rugs to absorb sound.

- Diffuse lighting and other visual stimulation where possible. Fluorescent lights can be covered with removable shades; consider having one area of the room with less lighting.

- Break activities and tasks into small steps. Use visual cue cards to show a child with autism what the steps look like one at a time. Allow time to practice.

- Provide a take-a-break space for all children, and especially for a child with autism who may need breaks from sensory input or social interactions. Take-a-break spaces should be low-sensory experiences, so a child can regroup and self-regulate.

- Keep a disability perspective. Remember that many challenging behaviors may come from a child with autism not understanding how to interact with others or not under-standing what feelings mean.

- Some children with autism benefit from a lower teacher–child ratio.

Speech and Communication

- Know how the child communicates at home. With permission from parents or guard-ians, talk to therapists who may be working with the child to incorporate the same communication strategies in your program. These might include sign language or picture communication systems.

- Use visual supports, such as choice cards that let a child with autism pick snack or the next activity. This strategy can prevent power struggles.

- Use first-then visual supports that have pictures of the desired task and the preferred activity or play. (First you do the desired task or activity, such as cleanup, then you get the toy or activity you prefer, like Lego blocks.)

- Teach with pictures and storyboards. Use photos with words whenever possible.

- Label your environment with pictures and words. Use clear bins with labels where possible so a child knows where everything is and where it goes at cleanup time.

- Use concrete visual methods to teach abstract ideas. Picture cards allow a concept to be seen as well as heard.

- Seek to understand a child with ASD. Challenging behaviors generally serve a function for the child, so examine the behavior to see what the child may be telling you.

Strategies that support the inclusion of children with autism are strategies that generally work well for all children in child care. For instance, using a daily picture schedule supports routines that build impulse control for everyone. A high-quality inclusive child care will already have in place an environment that supports children with ASD as well as children who are typically developing.

CHAPTER 8: CEREBRAL PALSY

Isabella uses a wheelchair, because she was born with cerebral palsy and she has difficulty standing. She has been in her child care center since she was two years old and is now in the preschool room. Because the classroom has wide aisles, she is able to navigate to every activity center without asking for help. All the toys are within her reach on the shelves, but sometimes if something is on the floor, a friend will get it for her. Her chair fits under the sensory table, which is her favorite place to play. She can't decide if she likes water play or sand play more. She loves to scoop and pour. She doesn't even realize it, but that is helping her hands and fingers get stronger.

Defining Cerebral Palsy

Cerebral palsy (CP) is a neurological disability caused by damage to the brain before, during, or after birth. It may be identified at birth or later, when developmental delays become apparent.

- Cerebral palsy is the most common motor disability in children.

- Cerebral palsy's impact on development can range from mild to severe.

- About 3 in 1,000 children have cerebral palsy.

- Congenital CP is caused by brain damage before or during birth and accounts for the majority of cases of children with CP.

- Other risk factors for cerebral palsy include low birth weight, prematurity, infections that affect the brain during infancy, and brain injury due to accident or abuse.

- To be given a diagnosis of cerebral palsy, injury to the brain must occur before age sixteen.

- Forty-one percent of children with cerebral palsy also have some form of seizure disorder.

- Different types of therapies are used to minimize and control the effects of CP on a child's day-to-day functions. They include speech therapy, occupational therapy, and physical therapy.

- There is no cure for cerebral palsy.

Characteristics of Children with Cerebral Palsy: Implications for Child Care

Children with cerebral palsy may have developmental delays in:

Physical and Motor Development A child with CP may have delays due to low or high muscle tone, poor reflexes, and fine- or gross-motor problems. The degree of impact varies from child to child. Some children will be nonambulatory and use wheelchairs. A piece of equipment called a stander allows a child with CP to participate in activities while standing.

Cognitive Development Children with CP may have mild to severe intellectual disabilities. Early interventions that increase movement, exploration, and learning opportunities for a child with CP can affect the extent of its impact on cognitive development.

Speech and Language Development Due to motor or cognitive difficulties, children with CP may have delayed speech that can be helped with speech therapy. With some types of CP, a child cannot use speech to communicate and may have limited movement, inhibiting the ability to gesture or sign. For this child, assistive technology can be an invaluable tool in communicating. Such technology includes computers, computer programs, and voice output machines.

Oral-Motor Development In a child with moderate to severe CP, there may be great difficulty in swallowing. This can be dangerous, as airways can become blocked. Muscle impairment in the face and neck can impair capabilities to eat, swallow normally, and in some cases, speak. There are treatment options for oral-motor dysfunction, including surgery.

Early educators need to have a complete picture of a child's health and developmental needs in order to provide high-quality care and learning services. In addition, caregivers should follow these guidelines for a child who has CP:

- Have a comprehensive and up-to-date health record for the child. Make sure everyone who works with the child has pertinent health information about feeding and other care needs.

- Understand how any specialized equipment operates. This includes wheelchairs, communication devices, standers, and feeding utensils. Training can come from therapists, health consultants, or parents.

- Let the other children know that adaptive equipment items are not toys. Explain that the equipment helps their friend with walking or talking.

- Know what the child's needs are for positioning and handling. Physical therapists can advise on the best way to lift a child or position in chairs, on toileting, and on other daily activities.

- Ask the child's parents or guardians for signed consent to talk to speech, occupational, and physical therapists as well any other professionals working with the child. Learn how therapies can be applied throughout the child care setting.

Red Flags for Cerebral Palsy

A child may be diagnosed with CP at birth. However, for young children who may have mild to moderate CP or who may be at risk for CP after birth, the following are general developmental red flags:

- Child feels very floppy when lifted or conversely, very stiff.

- Child's legs cross when picked up.

- Child older than six months does not roll over.

- Child older than nine months is not sitting without support.

- Child does not cross midlines.

- Child older than six months does not bring hands together.

- Child older than six months has difficulty bringing hands to mouth.

- Child favors one side when crawling or drags one side when crawling.

- Child older than eighteen months does not attempt to walk.

- Child has difficulties in balance.

- Child has infant reflexes that do not fade.

- Child misses major milestones across domains.

Practical Application: Strategies for Including Children with Cerebral Palsy

Young children with cerebral palsy can be successfully included in early education programs when environmental adaptations are made, along with accommodations for health and safety needs. Providers should partner with families and therapists to use the most effective inclusion strategies, such as the following:

- Talk with therapists for ideas to accommodate the child's fine- and gross-motor needs in child care. For instance, build up utensils with foam for easier handling, or add grips to crayons. Connect knobs to puzzles for easier use.

- Keep aisles free of objects that would hinder a child in a wheelchair.

- Look for loose rugs or other environmental obstacles that could harm a child who is not a steady walker.

- Remember that a wheelchair is a mobility device, not a limitation. Ensure that a child in a wheelchair participates in physical activities like dancing with streamers, yoga, or outside play.

- Provide access to activity centers by adjusting the height of tables or seating. Make sure a child with CP is able to reach toys independently.

- Learn the best positioning of the child during mealtimes. For optimum posture, feet need to be supported and the head kept at midline.

- Use nonskid pads to keep a child's plate in place at mealtime. These pads are also useful to prevent slippage of paper, scissors, and other play materials.

- Provide opportunities for a child with CP to make choices and manage materials. These opportunities promote movement and autonomy.

- Get at the child's eye level to make sure there are interesting things to see, and to find ways to engage learning that the child can see and reach.

- Provide opportunities for quiet spaces and social places for a child to self-regulate feelings and sensory influences.

- Involve the child in movement activities as much as possible. Floor exercises where all children can move freely can be part of morning play.

- Talk to therapists before trying anything new with a child who has motor impairments to ensure safety and proper positioning.

- Encourage involvement with peers. Let peers be classroom helpers. Build on each child's strengths, regardless of ability.

- Promote an atmosphere of encouragement and acceptance of children's differences.

> Gross- and fine-motor delays may occur without a diagnosis of cerebral palsy. It is important that you share developmental red flags with families, so the appropriate evaluation and diagnosis can be made. The child care provider's role is to share developmental information, never to offer a diagnosis. However, the informal assessment done by the early educator can be used in a formal assessment.

CHAPTER 9: DOWN SYNDROME

Jackson is three years old. He has been attending the Sunshine Child Care Center since he was nine months old. He moved from the infant room to the toddler room, and now he is in with the other active preschoolers. Jackson, who has Down syndrome, has difficulty building with blocks or Legos because of his lack of fine-motor skills. His friend Sam helps when Jackson can't put two pieces together. At mealtime, he sits in a chair that supports his posture so he can feed himself as everyone else does. Jackson needs help doing some things. His teacher says everyone needs help sometimes. For example, Sam sometimes needs help zipping his coat.

Defining Down Syndrome

Down syndrome is a developmental disability that occurs when a child has an extra chromosome in the nucleus of each body cell. Typically, the nucleus contains twenty-three pairs of chromosomes. Down syndrome happens when a person has an extra copy of the twenty-first pair. The extra chromosome affects every cell in the body. Down syndrome is present at birth, though not always identified when a child is born. Here are some facts about Down syndrome:

- Down syndrome is the most common genetic disorder.

- Down syndrome is a lifelong developmental disability.

- According to the National Down Syndrome Society (NDSS), Down syndrome affects 1 in 691 children.

- Down syndrome affects people from all races and socioeconomic levels.

- If a mother has a child with Down syndrome, her risk for having another child with Down syndrome increases to one in one hundred.

- The risk of having a child with Down syndrome increases after women reach forty years of age.

- Genetic testing prenatally and after the baby is born are used to diagnose Down syndrome.

- The cause of the extra chromosome is unknown.

- There is no cure for Down syndrome, though early intervention can influence developmental outcomes for a child.

Down syndrome is usually identified at birth or prenatally. An infant who has Down syndrome may have some or all of the following characteristics:

- Poor muscle control or low muscle tone

- Small head

- Flattened facial features

- Upward slant to the eyes

- Short fingers, small hands and feet

- Small or atypically-shaped ears

- A single crease in the palm of the hand

A doctor will confirm a diagnosis of Down syndrome with a blood test that checks for the extra chromosome. Under Part C of IDEA (for children from birth to two years old), services can begin at birth for a child who has any developmental delays.

Characteristics of Children with Down Syndrome: Implications for Child Care

A child with Down syndrome will have a unique personality, as all children have. The child will have varying degrees of developmental impacts from Down syndrome. These impacts can include the following:

Cognitive Development. A child with Down syndrome will have mild to moderate intellectual disabilities. Cognitive impairment will be specific to each child. With early intervention, many children gain typical speech and language skills.

Motor Development. Down syndrome causes weak muscle tone and delayed gross- and fine-motor development. Physical and occupational therapies help a child gain muscle tone. The earlier the intervention, the better the motor development will be.

Physical Health and Development. Children with Down syndrome may have heart defects, digestive issues, and greater risk for infectious disease. Down syndrome affects a child's immune system. Medical research has improved the health outcomes for people with Down syndrome, including a longer life expectancy.

Social Development. Children with Down syndrome may have behavioral challenges and may lack social competencies. It is a myth that all children with Down syndrome have happy dispositions. A child with Down syndrome has a unique personality with behaviors similar to those of peers. A child needs skill building to understand concepts that are important both to friendships and to staying safe.

Young children with Down syndrome are usually delayed in reaching typical developmental milestones. They may develop speech later or may always have some speech and language difficulty. Since muscle tone is affected, a child may take longer to sit up, crawl, or walk. In addition, some children with Down syndrome will exhibit challenging behaviors. This may be due to delays in cognitive and speech development. When children do not understand expectations, they can become frustrated.

The early childhood educator can be successful at including a child with Down syndrome by asking parents and guardians the following questions:

- Does your child have any current medical concerns?

- Has your child had recent surgery I need to know about?

- Does your child have any physical limitations?

- Is your child working with any therapists? Are there specific strategies I could embed into activities in child care that support your child's therapy goals?

- What adaptations work at home that would also work at child care?

- How does your child prefer to sleep? What foods does your child prefer to eat? Is there anything your child has problems eating?

- What are your child's toileting needs? How much assistance is needed from the teacher?

- How does your child like to play? How does your child interact with peers?

- How does your child communicate best?

- How does your child make friends?

- Are there any specific behaviors I should know about? How do you guide behavior?

Red Flags for Down Syndrome

Children with Down syndrome have distinct physical characteristics usually observable at birth. A child care provider will want to make careful ongoing observations of the following to ensure positive developmental outcomes:

- Delayed speech or speech difficulties

- Poor functioning with fine-motor skills in eating or in self-care like dressing

- Gross-motor delays in sitting up, crawling, walking, or running

- Difficulties after eating and complaining of stomachaches or heartburn

- Persistent tantrums

- Hearing loss or change in hearing ability

- Withdrawing behaviors

Practical Application: Strategies for Including Children with Down Syndrome

Strategies for including children with Down syndrome should incorporate accommodations in the physical environment as well as in activities. Many of these strategies work well in a setting with all children. They include the following:

- Work with families and specialists to learn how best to embed developmental goals into everyday experiences at child care.

- Encourage engagement of infants in the environment around them by talking, singing, cooing, and using favorite objects to get and keep their attention.

- Provide opportunities for infants to explore their surroundings, reach and grab toys, and turn their heads while watching objects near them move.

- Provide a variety of learning opportunities, including sensory experiences.

- Teach with visuals. Have directions for a task broken into visual steps. Use a visual cue card for transitions.

- If a child is not yet speaking, ask the family what signs they use for objects and incorporate the signs into your program. Help other children learn the signs.

- For a child who is nonambulatory or not walking independently, keep space clear of obstacles and have toys at an accessible level.

- Provide opportunities to practice self-help skills like zippering or buttoning.

- Encourage fine-motor skills in play by stacking, building, using crayons, and using puzzles with knobs.

- Learn how best to position a child for play, eating, or resting.

- Motivate a child to do more physically by providing a preferred toy or object that the child can grasp or crawl toward. Work on physical skills when a child is well rested and has energy.

Keep a disability perspective. A child with Down syndrome may master milestones later than peers, but it is important to include the child in all activities to promote mastery.

CHAPTER 10: FETAL ALCOHOL SPECTRUM DISORDER

Jeremiah, who is four years old, has been enrolled in his preschool for eight months. He likes to go to preschool, but he sometimes has difficulty understanding rules. He also struggles with transitions from his favorite play activities. His teacher knows he has a fetal alcohol spectrum disorder (FASD) diagnosis, and she is working closely with his special education teacher to give him the structure he needs in her classroom.

Defining Fetal Alcohol Spectrum Disorder

Fetal alcohol spectrum disorder is an umbrella term that describes the range of effects that can occur in a child whose mother drank alcohol during pregnancy. Here are some important facts about FASD:

- The brain is the most important organ damaged by alcohol.

- FASD is 100 percent preventable if a woman does not drink during pregnancy.

- FASD is the number one preventable cause of intellectual disability.

- There is no known safe amount of alcohol to drink during pregnancy.

- There is no known safe time during pregnancy to drink alcohol.

- One in ten pregnant women report alcohol consumption.

- Unplanned pregnancy is a contributing factor to FASD, because mothers who drink alcohol on a regular basis may not be aware they are pregnant until birth defects have already occurred.

- Alcohol affects different parts of an infant's development during different stages of pregnancy.

- The effects of FASD on a child may include physical, cognitive, behavioral, and learning disabilities.

- Some children are born with distinct FASD physical characteristics, but other children show only the cognitive and behavioral impairments of FASD.

- There is no cure for FASD.

Health professionals will diagnose FASD in children using evaluation checklists in four major areas (MOFAS 2010):

- Growth: This refers to a child's overall physical growth and development compared to peers of the same age. A child with FASD will generally be smaller and develop physically at a slower rate than peers.

- Facial features: Children with FASD may have distinct facial characteristics, such as a wider space between the nose and upper lip, a thin upper lip, and a smooth philtrum (the groove between the nose and upper lip).

- Brain development and functioning: FASD may cause cognitive deficits and developmental delays determined through IQ testing and other testing. Some children with FASD struggle with cause and effect, reasoning, and impulse control.

- Exposure to alcohol: A maternal history of alcohol use during pregnancy strengthens the case for a diagnosis of FASD when other factors are also present.

Characteristics of Children with Fetal Alcohol Spectrum Disorder: Implications for Child Care

Children with FASD will have varying impacts of the disability on their cognitive, physical, and behavioral development. It is important to work in partnership with professionals who are serving the children as well as with the families. Behavioral characteristics of FASD may be the most difficult for child care providers to manage. Typical guidance strategies are not consistently effective with a child who has FASD. Also, remember that one strategy might work today but not tomorrow. The child care environment plays a major role in behavioral interventions. Structure and routine are necessary for a child who may be poorly regulated. Sensory stimulation can overarouse a child with FASD, who may have sensory processing issues.

Limitations and boundaries are tools in the environment to promote greater attention spans and lessen impulsive behaviors. Physical boundaries can include shelves to partition activity areas. Tape can be used to show a child where activities begin or end. Rules give a child a sense of structure and consistency.

When working with children who have FASD, keep these concepts in mind:

- Because a child with FASD may be easily overstimulated and difficult to soothe, it is important that the early education environment have take-a-break spaces, be designed with quiet areas next to quiet areas (such as art next to reading), and use sound-muffling strategies to control noise (such as using carpet in high-traffic areas or using shelving to act as a natural boundary).

- Children with FASD have poor impulse control and may react with inappropriate behaviors. Be aware of what triggers a child's overreactions and lessen the impact if possible. Some things that might bother a child could include inconsistent and unstructured environments, big open spaces, new or unexpected changes in the schedule, fatigue, or hunger.

- Expect regressions in development for children with FASD. Avoid blaming children or saying, "You could do this yesterday." They may be inconsistent in performing skills they could do earlier. This is part of the disability.

- The more children with FASD can practice impulse control and regulation, the more positive the outcomes for them throughout their lives. FASD is a lifetime disability, but early interventions can help a child learn social norms and appropriate behaviors.

Red Flags for Fetal Alcohol Spectrum Disorder

Here some general red flags that may indicate a child should be evaluated for FASD:

- Sleep difficulties

- Irritability

- Self-regulation difficulty

- Poor coordination

- Delayed fine- and gross-motor development

- Sensory difficulties

- Extreme tantrums

- Lack of stranger anxiety, poor social boundaries

- Difficulty sharing and cooperating; playing alone rather than with peers

- Hyperactivity and high impulsivity

- Poor attention skills

- Poor reasoning and memorization skills

Many of these red flags are common in children at different ages and stages. Behaviors listed above could be part of a child's dominant temperament traits. They are also common in children with other types of behavioral and developmental disabilities. It is important when observing and recording that the early educator indicate frequency, duration, and settings where behaviors are seen. Parents who are referred to early intervention can use the informal assessment as background information for making an accurate formal assessment and diagnosis.

Practical Application: Strategies for Including Children with Fetal Alcohol Spectrum Disorder

Because of the nature of their neurological damage, children with FASD may present challenges to a child care program that are different from those presented by other children with disabilities. Guidance strategies need to be specific to the impact of FASD on impulse control, self-regulation, and the inability of children to realize cause and effect. Knowing that the brain of a child with FASD responds differently to behavior interventions can mean more effective strategies for child care teachers. Following are some recommended strategies:

- Provide concrete rewards and consequences. Subtle rewards, such as praise or natural consequences, may be hard for children with FASD to relate to their actions.

- Provide choice and encourage decision making. Visual choice cards may be useful if children have any speech and language delays.

- Establish consistent routines. Use a daily picture schedule and refer to it throughout the day. Children with FASD may benefit from personal picture schedules that they carry with them.

- Use simple rules and enforce with simple language. Consequences and rewards need to be immediate.

- Teach new skills in small pieces; break directions into small steps. Reinforce as a child completes each step.

- Teach with concrete language. Use visuals as much as possible to represent what is being taught.

- Provide a wait time for children to process language, depending on their speech and language needs.

- Watch for signs of overstimulation. Intervene before children get overaroused and difficult to calm or regulate. Help children know their own body signs for overstimulation, like feeling their heartbeat and recognizing whether it is fast or slow.

- Practice tools for regulating, like deep breathing.

- Do not hesitate to repeat, repeat, repeat. A child with FASD may have short- or long-term memory problems. Information may need to be provided many times.

> Because a child's maternal history of alcohol use may be unknown or not disclosed, and a child may not have distinct facial features of FASD, it may be incorrectly diagnosed as another type of developmental disability. Valuable time can be lost in reaping the benefits of early intervention specific to the needs of a child with FASD.

CHAPTER 11: FINE- AND GROSS-MOTOR DELAYS

Geneva and Justine are three-year-old twins who were born twelve weeks premature. While Justine is meeting typical milestones in her motor development, Geneva, who has been diagnosed with cerebral palsy, is not yet confident in her running and climbing. She likes to hold her teacher's hand when they walk on the uneven pebbles on the playground outside. Justine will sometimes run ahead of her sister to get to the outdoor slide at preschool but then turn and wait for Geneva to catch up so they can go together.

Defining Fine- and Gross-Motor Development

Motor development is continuous from prebirth to adolescence. Here are some basic facts about motor development:

- Gross-motor development refers to the use of the large muscles of the neck, trunk, arms, and legs.

- Fine-motor development refers to movement of the smaller muscles in the hands, fingers, feet, and toes.

- In typical development, gross- and fine-motor development should work in tandem.

In order for physical development to follow a sequential pattern, certain characteristics need to be in place:

- Motor development depends on normal muscle tone.

- Muscle tone refers to the degree of tension in a muscle when it is at rest.

- When a child has low or high muscle tone due to a disability, gross-motor development can be delayed or inhibited.

- Hypotonic muscles have low tone. Hypotonic muscles make it difficult to maintain control of posture.

- Hypertonic muscles have high tone. Hypertonic muscles are tense and may be resistant to sudden, passive movement.

- Children who are hypotonic or hypertonic will need physical therapy and specific exercises to decrease or increase their muscle tone.

- Typical motor development moves from head to foot and from the middle of the body outward. Children hold their heads up before they roll. The trunk develops first, and development progresses outward to the limbs.

Developmental milestones build on one another, and mastery is needed before a child can move forward in development. For example, infants must learn to roll over and sit up before they can pull themselves to standing. Walking occurs before running. Here is how the process works, on a basic level:

- Motor development relies on an intact sensory system, which enables movement.

- The sensory system brings information to children through their movement, helping them learn where their body is in relation to space.

- The child's sensory system takes input from the environment and integrates it in a way that helps the child learn how to move.

Characteristics of Children with Motor Disabilities: Implications for Child Care

Young children develop physically at uneven rates. There are ranges in the expectations for children regarding when they will sit up, stand, or walk. A motor delay occurs when the typical developmental expectations are not being met and the child needs intervention in order to continue along a gross- and fine-motor development trajectory. Following are some key causes of motor disabilities:

- Gross- and fine-motor delays may be part of a child's disability or may be from unknown causes.

- Genetic disorders such as Down syndrome, muscular dystrophy, and fragile X syndrome can affect a child's ongoing physical development.

- Brain injury before, during, or after birth, including traumatic brain injury, illness, abuse, or accident, can cause motor delays.

- Disabilities like cerebral palsy affect overall motor development to varying degrees.

- Exposure to toxins such as lead, alcohol, mercury, and pesticides before and after birth can cause neurological damage. This affects brain development, which in turn affects physical and motor development.

Whatever the cause, a motor disability will be characterized by a pattern of delayed development and/or differences that make performance of a particular skill a more difficult task. Motor disabilities may play out in a variety of ways:

- The impact of the delay may be in fine-motor skills rather than gross-motor skills. For example, a young child may be able to sit up in a preschool chair but may have difficulty grasping a spoon or holding a glass.

- A motor delay may accompany other delays, such as speech and language delays or cognitive impairments.

- To the early childhood educator, a motor delay may be a signal of other kinds of developmental concerns that have not been assessed yet, such as a learning disability or other neurological disorders.

Red Flags for a Motor Delay

Armed with child development knowledge and ongoing observation and recording of a child's progression, the early childhood professional plays an important role in recognizing early signs of motor delay. In general, look for these red flags:

- Stiffness and rigidity or floppiness like a rag doll

- Overall clumsiness, tripping, or excessive falling

- Avoidance of fine-motor activities

- Abnormal positioning of arms or legs at playtime or naptime

- No reaching across body during play

- Reaching consistently with only one hand

- Crawling while dragging one side of the body

- Inability to control body movements, including jerking or spasms

- Significant difference in skills between left and right sides of the body (arms and legs)

- Any loss or regression in skills

Some specific red flags at different development ages might include:

- Cannot hold head steady by four months

- Does not roll over at six months

- Does not bear weight on legs by seven months

- Does not bring objects to mouth by nine months

- Is not crawling or pulling to stand by twelve months

- Is not walking or using a spoon or cup by eighteen months

- Does not walk steadily or throw a ball by age two

- Is falling a lot or can't use simple manipulatives by age three

Be familiar with typical child development. The Centers for Disease Control and Prevention's web page "Learn the Signs. Act Early." is a comprehensive resource for typical development and developmental red flags.

Practical Application: Strategies for Including Children with Motor Delays

Children with fine- and gross-motor delays can be included in a child care setting when the environment is set up for their success. Each child will have individual needs, but most children with motor difficulties will benefit from these general adaptations:

- Ensure that the child care space is set up for children to move around easily. Be aware of any barriers that block access for a child in a wheelchair or who may be unsteady when walking or reaching. Watch for slippery rugs or larger items, such as bikes, that a child might have to walk around.

- Promote independence for a child with motor delays by keeping toys and activities accessible. Keep shelves at a height that a child who is in a wheelchair could reach.

- As much as possible, design activities so a child does not have to ask for teacher assistance to complete them. If a child has difficulty holding a paintbrush, provide opportunities for fingerpainting. Some children will benefit from grips being added to pencils, crayons, and so on. Grips can be purchased or made from foam tubing.

- Match equipment to the children's needs. Make sure the table for meals or activities can be adjusted for a wheelchair. Lower the sensory table so a child can reach it from a sitting position. Assess what children can see from their level and adapt the environment so each child can see and touch interesting things.

- Let children practice. Give opportunities for a child with fine-motor delays to play with the manipulatives so the child can improve skills such as grasping and picking up.

- As much as possible, give children time to finish their play and their jobs.

- Encourage self-feeding to promote eye–hand coordination, even when it takes a bit longer.

- Take time to learn about any adaptive equipment that a child may use. Children with motor delays may have braces, walkers, or wheelchairs, or they may use a bolster or wedge when sitting or lying down.

- Work with families and therapists so you can use equipment to promote optimal support. Make sure that any larger equipment the child needs for standing or sitting fits in areas where the child wants to be (such as the dramatic play center and the art center).

- Involve families. Strategies that work at home may be useful in the child care setting. Ask families how they make adaptations for feeding, dressing, and other daily skills.

- Plan physical activities for parts of the day when a child with motor delays has the most energy. Help the child be successful.

- Use simple songs with fingerplays to encourage fine-motor skills.

- Involve all the children in inclusion. Pair a child who has strong social skills as a play partner with a child who might need assistance or more time to complete activities.

- Give plenty of positive encouragement when a child is trying to accomplish a difficult goal. Don't let children think you doubt they can do something. No one knows the potential of any young child, so encourage children to try new activities, and experiment with adaptations to get them there.

> Early childhood practitioners are not diagnosticians and do not make assessments of disabilities. In sharing developmental concerns with families, it is important not to make reference to any given disability, since that is not the role of the early educator. However, knowing the signs of motor delay can help you record objective developmental observations. You can share these with families in order to benefit the children.

CHAPTER 12: HEARING IMPAIRMENT

Kou is playing with his favorite truck next to his friend Christian. They are hauling blocks on a make-believe highway. Kou gestures for Christian to load up his truck with more blocks until it is full. While Kou is hard of hearing, he and his friend communicate easily with signs and gestures while they play side by side.

Defining Hearing Impairment

A hearing impairment occurs when there is damage to the outer, middle, or inner ear that affects ear function. The damage affects the receiving or processing of sound vibrations. Children with hearing loss may be either profoundly deaf, meaning they cannot process spoken language, or hard of hearing, which refers to a less significant loss (Allen and Cowdery 2012). Following are some key facts about hearing impairment:

- All hearing loss affects development in infants and young children.

- Hearing loss can be present at birth due to congenital birth defect or maternal illness.

- The CDC reports that about 50 percent of hearing loss in children is due to genetics (CDC 2015).

- Hearing impairment can also be acquired after birth through illness, injury, or environmental hazards.

- Intermittent or mild hearing loss can occur in childhood from frequent ear infections and wax buildup.

- Hearing loss can be mild to severe as well as temporary or intermittent.

Many newborns undergo simple screening tests that measure normal hearing function. Here are some concepts to keep in mind with regard to hearing screening:

- The CDC recommends a hearing screening before one month of age.

- If there appears to be a developmental delay in hearing as a child grows, or if a hearing problem is discovered in a preschool screening, an audiologist will conduct hearing tests to determine loss or impairment.

- Infants and young children identified with hearing impairment may be eligible for services under the IDEA.

- Some children will benefit from devices like hearing aids or surgically inserted cochlear implants.

- Children may learn American Sign Language (ASL) or cued speech to communicate with others.

- ASL is considered its own language with unique movements and sentence structures (ASHA 2016).

Characteristics of Children with Hearing Impairment: Implications for Child Care

The earlier hearing impairment is identified, the better are the outcomes for children in speech and language development, social skills, and cognitive development.

Language Development The developmental domain most affected by hearing loss is language. Even a mild hearing loss that goes undetected can result in a lack of language development that puts a child at risk for developmental delay. A child who is not identified with hearing loss at birth or who acquires an unidentified hearing loss later will lose ground on the imitation of sounds, words, tone, and other important language skills. These may be remediated with a speech and language pathologist depending on the child's hearing needs.

Cognitive Development If speech and language development are delayed by hearing loss, cognitive development will be affected. Children's cognitive development can be affected to the degree that their lack of language skills prevents them from understanding the many types of teaching going on around them. Learning may become difficult if the hearing impairment is not recognized right away or if interventions for hearing are not successfully implemented. For instance, children who hear only parts of what a teacher is saying when giving directions are not going to be able to complete a task successfully. Children may not even realize what they are missing. The teacher, not recognizing the hearing loss, may become frustrated with the lack of follow-through on a child's part, creating a cycle of negativity for the child.

Social Development Social development can also be impaired if a child does not have a way to communicate with peers, either through spoken language or through adaptations to speech, such as signing or gestures. Children who are deaf may be left out by friends if they cannot engage in reciprocal conversation for play or activities. A child who has impairments may feel isolated and withdraw socially.

Red Flags for Hearing Impairment

The American Speech-Language-Hearing Association reports that 4 to 6 percent of children who have hearing loss develop the impairment between birth and six years of age (ASHA 2016). It is likely that an early educator will notice red flags for hearing loss through the day-to-day interactions with a child. Early intervention is key to better outcomes for a child with hearing loss, so helping families find an appropriate referral to services is critical.

Here are some general red flags for a child who may be experiencing hearing loss:

- Does not startle at loud noise

- Does not turn toward sounds

- As an infant, does not vocalize different sounds

- Does not learn language

- Does not understand or respond to name

- Uses no simple words, such as *no* or *mama*

- Hears some sounds but not others

- Babbled early on but then stopped

- Can't tell where a sound is coming from

- Has delayed speech or speech is difficult to understand

- Appears to not understand directions

- Follows through with some instructions and not others (as though missing part of conversation)

- Nods and smiles when spoken to but doesn't answer specific questions

- Withdraws socially

- Acts out with challenging behaviors

It may be hard to recognize mild hearing impairments in children without careful ongoing observation of development. Having concrete and nonjudgmental information to share with families will help them make the best decisions about evaluation.

Practical Application: Strategies for Including Children with Hearing Impairment

The early childhood environment is a critical tool in successfully including a child with hearing impairment. Here are some strategies for the setting:

- Keep the child with hearing loss close to you during group time or activities. Be sure the child is near enough to hear your voice clearly.

- Use an amplification system in the classroom. A microphone that the teacher uses can transmit to a child's earpiece, giving the child higher volume of sound.

- Keep noise distractions in the classroom to a minimum. Listen for what is going on in your program.

- Look for ways to muffle sound, such as using shelving as boundaries for activities or using carpet to absorb sound.

- Label the environment with words and picture cards. Put toys in clear bins with labels.

- Teach with visuals. As much as possible, use visual representations of concepts you are teaching.

- Use a visual picture schedule with words and pictures of the activities.

Other adaptations for a child with hearing impairment can be made in teacher-to-child and child-to-peer relationships. Here are some examples:

- Get at the child's eye level when speaking to the child.

- Speak clearly and give the child time to process. Use normal tones when speaking.

- Give directions one step at a time. Make sure you know the child is tuned in to you before giving instructions.

- Have a physical or visual cue for the child that indicates when you need the child's attention. This could be as simple as a yellow circle or a hand on the child's shoulder.

- Follow the interventions used at home and with therapists (with family consent).

- Learn signs for basic words if American Sign Language is being used. Post basic signs around the program for everyone to learn.

- Enlist the child's family. What works at home may work in the child care setting. Find out how family members help the child make choices at home.

- Ensure that the child feels a sense of belonging and is included in all the activities within the program.

Hearing loss will affect children differently depending on when it occurs. A child who is born deaf will not have the benefit of hearing sounds in order to learn language. If hearing is lost after a child has begun using speech, therapists can build on existing language skills. It is important that the early childhood educator be in partnership with the child's specialists in order to build on strategies that will enhance communication, whether that means learning signs or embedding ways to practice sounds into daily child care activities. These strategies could include reading books, rhyming, and singing songs that practice letters or sounds.

Parents and guardians have the final word on what interventions a child will have for hearing loss. If the family chooses sign language, teachers can learn signs for basic words and help the other children learn them as well.

It is crucial that a child who has hearing impairment be given every opportunity to build relationships with peers. Playing with others will help build language as well as social and cognitive skills. It can be easy for a child with hearing impairment to become isolated from others who don't understand the child or who get frustrated with communication.

Teachers can support successful play by sitting next to the child with hearing loss during play and by modeling play skills until the child is comfortable. It is important that adults give children without hearing loss ways to communicate with children who have hearing loss. These techniques could be gestures if a child is deaf, or showing children how to speak clearly and directly to the child who has hearing loss. Peers of the child with a disability will look to the early educator as the role model.

> The early educator, through observation and recording, may find a pattern of red flags in a child with hearing loss, making referral to early intervention possible. Once an evaluation has been made and services have begun for hearing impairment, the child care professional can work with the speech and language specialists or other specialists to embed therapies in the daily routines of child care.

CHAPTER 13: SENSORY PROCESSING DISORDER

Mi, who is five, has been in Ms. Sandy's family child care program for five months. Ms. Sandy has noticed that by the middle of the afternoon, Mi sometimes can't calm herself down to play with a peer. This can result in a conflict with her friends during a game or in the dramatic play area. She seems over-energized and not able to manage all her emotions. Ms. Sandy is going to work on creating a quiet space for Mi and others who may need to take breaks during the day to get away from sensory overload. Mi needs help in getting her engine to run slower, and Miss Sandy wants to find tools to help her.

Defining Sensory Processing Disorder

Sensory processing is the brain's ability to receive information through the senses and interpret that information throughout the day in order to learn, function, and survive. Sensory information helps us organize our behavior so we can explore, interact, and navigate successfully within our different environments. Sensory processing disorder (SPD) occurs when our brain does not properly interpret information coming in through our senses. It is an inability to respond appropriately to ordinary and everyday sensory experiences.

If children are overresponsive, they will be sensory avoiding in one or more of their senses. If children are underresponsive, they will be sensory seeking, or looking for input. Here are some basic facts to know about SPD:

- Sensory processing disorder is a spectrum disorder, which means it has a wide range of impacts on different children.

- No child with SPD will look the same as another child with SPD.

- Some children may have sensory issues in only one sense, and others may have problems in multiple senses.

- A child can be overresponsive and underresponsive at the same time.

- The exact cause of SPD, like other neurological disorders, is unknown.

- SPD is most commonly diagnosed in young children, though adults may discover SPD as an explanation for lifelong challenges.

- Studies indicate that SPD affects as many as one in twenty children in daily life (SPD Foundation 2016).

- If children are born prematurely, their sensory systems will likely be immature and will take longer to develop.

- Other disabilities often coexist with SPD.

- Illness and other medical issues can have short- and long-term effects on a child's sensory system. This includes hospitalization, during which a child experiences less sensory stimulation.

- Environmental toxins such as lead and mercury, as well as other neurotoxins, have been linked to SPD.

- Family stressors can increase a child's sensitivities.

- Once a child is identified with SPD, the child can work with an occupational therapist to foster appropriate and typical responses to everyday sensory experiences.

- The goal will be to help the child have more functional skills in any setting to learn, play, and interact with others.

Characteristics of Children with Sensory Processing Disorder: Implications for Child Care

SPD is often difficult to discover in a young child, because all children are developing regulatory skills and personal preferences according to their temperaments. Two-year-olds have less ability to control the impulse to bite someone when they want something in their mouths than older children have. A three-year-old who has poor regulation skills due to a low sensory threshold as part of the child's natural temperament may occasionally use aggression to meet a need. However, three-year-olds generally should use greater impulse control than toddlers do because three-year-olds have greater language and communication skills. Differences in sensory needs can lead to challenges in child care, so keep these guidelines in mind:

- It is important that the child care environment be set up in a way that promotes self-regulation and a sense of security through consistency, routine, and responsive caregiving.

- If the adults are comfortable with noise and high activity levels, children who are reactive to sound or have a strong need for routine will struggle to manage their sensory needs.

- A child may use challenging behaviors to get removed from the noise, which may frustrate child care staff members if they are unaware of the environmental impact on the child's sensory needs.

- A child care provider who is more sedate in activity level may struggle with a child who is trying to gain sensory input through gross-motor movement, such as running and jumping.

- Awareness of your own dominant temperament traits, such as intensity, persistence, regulation, and sensitivity, can help you ensure a good fit for all children, regardless of their sensory needs.

There are seven senses in the human sensory system. Each sense plays a unique role in how we take in information from the world around us in order to learn, be safe, and continue developing. Each sense has implications for child care if a child is sensory-seeking or sensory-avoiding in any of these areas:

Visual Sense Our eyes provide us with information through sight. We learn much about our environment through what we see. Young children are affected by color, lighting, clutter, and other visual stimuli. A child who underreacts visually may seek input by playing with toys that light up. Conversely, a child who overresponds visually may be distracted by visual stimulation and use behaviors to avoid an area that has too much going on visually to process.

Auditory Sense Our ears give us information through hearing. We all have a sensory threshold for how much sound we can manage before it bothers us. For a child with auditory processing issues, the everyday sounds of ten preschoolers in a classroom laughing and talking can be overwhelming. Children who are overresponsive to sounds may put their hands over their ears when the noise is too much or may have trouble paying attention when the environment is loud. Children who are underresponsive to sounds may seek out noisy toys and games or turn music up loud. They will be seeking louder sounds than children typically seek.

Gustatory Sense Our mouths provide us with information through taste. Children may be picky eaters because of the texture or taste of food. They may avoid strong flavors if they are overresponsive or seek out stronger flavors if they are underresponsive. For instance, a child might often say, "This is too spicy," or, on the other hand, might want to add salt to everything.

Olfactory Sense Our noses give us information through our sense of smell. All of us have odors we do not like and fragrances that appeal to us. In a child with disordered olfactory processing, smells may disrupt concentration. A child might complain about smells that an adult can't even smell. A child who is overresponsive might protest going into the lunch area if tacos are being served, because the smell is overwhelming. A child who is underresponsive might seek out odors, looking for things with strong smells.

Tactile Sense The surface of our skin provides us with information about shape, size, and texture of objects in our environment through our sense of touch. This sense also tells us if we are touching something or if it is touching us. It helps us distinguish between touch that is threatening and touch that is nonthreatening. A child who is overresponsive to tactile stimulation may protest putting on a certain shirt or pair of socks or touching certain materials in the activity centers. A child who is underresponsive may touch everything, including other children, when waiting in line or at the snack table. This may be the child who needs to have a blanket or animal close by, especially when stressed.

Vestibular Sense Our inner ears give us information about equilibrium, movement, gravity, space, and where our body is in relation to the world around us through our sense of balance. Swinging, running, riding a bike, rocking, and spinning give input to this sense. A child who is underresponsive in the vestibular sense will seek input through moving, swinging, and spinning. The child will seem to have no fear when playing on the gross-motor equipment. A child who is overresponsive will act in the opposite way, avoiding movement that is unsettling or puts one off balance. The child may want to hold hands with an adult when walking on uneven ground or climbing stairs.

Proprioceptive Sense Our muscles, joints, and ligaments provide us with information about where our body parts are (body awareness) and help us coordinate movement through proprioception. This is also referred to as our muscle sense. Children who are overresponsive in their proprioceptive sense will avoid physical activity if they feel insecure about falling or being hurt. They may seem clumsy to others. If they are underresponsive, they may run into things, hug too hard, break crayons because they push down too hard, or want to wrestle with others to receive input to their muscles and joints.

Each of the seven senses influences how a young child will learn and act in a child care environment. Once a child is assessed with SPD, the environment can be adapted to meet the child's needs for more or less sensory stimulation.

Red Flags for Sensory Processing Disorder

We all have sensory preferences. A preference is simply what we like better. We have different levels of noise that we prefer as well as foods that we like and dislike. A sensory preference becomes dysregulated only when it interferes with learning, relating to others, or general life functions.

The following are examples of red flags for SPD:

- A child may have developmental delays in gross-motor or fine-motor skills. Watch for unusual patterns of development, lack of skills typical for a child's age, or loss of skills. A child may avoid some activities, like running or climbing, if they are difficult. A child with fine-motor delays may avoid using scissors.

- A child may have behaviors that are atypical for the child's age, such as avoiding play with peers or avoiding certain activities. Children may avoid outside play if they are afraid of falling or avoid the block area if the lighting bothers their eyes.

- Children may have emotional outbursts or tantrums at changes in programming or in the environment. It might look like these children are simply exhibiting challenging behaviors, but the purpose of the behaviors may be to avoid situations that cause sensory aversion. Maybe the gym is so loud that the children know they will react badly, so they use behavior that will keep them out of the gym.

- Very low energy (avoiding behaviors) or very high energy (seeking behaviors) may be a clue about sensory processing. Children who withdraw may be saying that they have reached their maximum for interaction. They may need a low-sensory take-a-break space. Children who won't stop running may be saying that their muscles need input. They could be encouraged to march around the room instead.

Here are red flag areas around specific behaviors:

Self-Regulation Children begin to master self-regulation as a social-emotional milestone at age three. In preschoolers, some impulse-control problems will be expected, because they are learning compromise and problem-solving skills. Preschoolers who often have tantrums or meltdowns are having trouble regulating their emotions. Children who hit other children in line may be overstimulated by touch, their proximity to others, or the noise of the transition and therefore cannot regulate their bodies. Self-regulation expectations for a toddler are much lower than for a preschooler with typical speech and language ability.

Appropriate Level of Arousal Children have a smaller window than adults have for calm, alert, and organized arousal states, because their sensory systems are less sophisticated. Younger children have fewer tools for managing their arousal levels, so expectations should be different for infants, toddlers, and preschoolers. Red flags for SPD could include an infant who cannot settle into sleep without great difficulty, a toddler who cries and cannot be consoled but does not appear to be hurt or afraid, or a preschooler who is withdrawn and cannot be engaged easily in play.

Attention to Task An older child who cannot finish activities or follow directions may need sensory input or may be reacting to sensory information overload. Observing when and where this occurs can give clues to sensory influences on the behavior.

Frustration Tolerance The age of the child determines what is developmentally appropriate for handling frustration. A child who is frequently frustrated by naturally occurring events, such as wait times, the need to share, and transitions, may be having a sensory reaction.

Practical Application: Strategies for Including Children with Sensory Processing Disorder

It is often difficult to distinguish whether a child has sensory processing disorder or is simply more sensitive to the environment than the typical child. Moreover, other disabilities, such as ADHD, autism, and fetal alcohol spectrum disorder, can include sensory issues such as over- or underresponsiveness to sensory input. In addition, sensory processing disorder may coexist with other disabilities so that a child has multiple diagnoses. If a child does not have a known disability, observation and recording of behaviors will show a picture of the child's needs that can be shared with the family. The family can use information gathered in child care for formal assessment. Regardless of diagnosis, you can apply the following general prevention and intervention strategies:

Prevention Strategies

Regulation Development Establish routines and rules. Every time you follow a schedule, you build the child's internal biological regulatory system. Regulation is the key to helping a child with sensory issues.

Visual Cues, Schedules, and Timers These are tools that help build regulatory skills in children. A timer in an activity center helps give a child a sense of time. It can prevent over-response by a child who does not want to leave an activity to go somewhere less preferred. Schedules build regulation, which helps a child control impulses.

Social Skills Instruction It is helpful for children who struggle with regulation to know words for their emotions so they can tell you or their peers what they are feeling. This can prevent aggression or conflict. Older children can practice social skills in role play or in skits that they help write.

Choice Chart and First-Then Chart You can sometimes prevent challenging behaviors by limiting the decisions that a child with regulatory challenges has to make. A choice chart gives a child two choices at a time for a given activity, snack, or play area. A first-then chart (first you do this task, then you can do something you prefer) is another visual support that offers children choices and helps build self-regulation.

Quiet Area for Breaks Quiet take-a-break spaces help children regulate themselves when they begin to feel overwhelmed by sensory influences or peer interactions. Such spaces help children regroup and calm themselves from high arousal to alert and organized.

Opportunities for Movement Have children march or move in another creative way from one activity to another. Moving the body to rhythm and giving input to the feet can be regulating. Allow opportunities for movement, such as a game of musical chairs or skating on paper plates, before and after quiet activities.

Meals Give children food choices when possible; avoid power struggles over specific foods when similar foods are available. Keep portions small if you are unsure whether children will eat something or if you are introducing something new.

> Take a disability perspective when possible. Remember that SPD is a neurological condition and not simply a child being obstinate or trying to ruin your day.

Intervention Strategies

Fidgets Keep handy a basket full of Koosh balls and other sensory toys. These can help a child who may be needing to touch something, especially during a transition or wait time.

Clear Instructions Children who are easily overwhelmed or distracted by sounds in the room or other sensory stimulation will be more successful completing a task if they are given one step at a time. If the task or activity is a frequent one, consider creating a visual of all the steps for children to use.

Specific Praise Tell children when they have been successful, even in small ways. Build on their success. Let them know specifically what they did that followed a rule or a direction.

Encouragement (Verbal and Nonverbal) Encourage children by letting them know they are on task or are using feeling words. A smile at the right time can help children realize they are on the right track—and continue on it.

Planned Transitions A child with sensory challenges may have more difficulty than other children in moving from one activity to another or from one setting to another. If you are planning a field trip, talk about it ahead of time. Use a picture schedule for the day of the field trip. For daily transitions, have wait time activities planned. Use a cue for a child who struggles with change, such as a yellow cue card for cleanup time.

Environment Offer a comfortable learning space without distractions. Put quiet centers by quiet centers, such as the art area near the reading area. Avoid bright lights and bright colors. Limit auditory and visual stimuli in the environment. Be creative in offering personal space to children. Create personal space at tables using cookie sheets, trays, place mats, or electrical tape. Use colored tape to visually designate personal space when lining up at the door, when waiting at the drinking fountain, or during group meetings. Offer a variety of seating options for floor time, such as cushions, carpet squares, and cube chairs.

In child care, we never diagnose conditions or tell families what disorder or disability their children may have. We share pertinent, objective observations on development so families can make decisions about assessment and evaluation. With SPD, we will likely be sharing red flags around a variety of behaviors. These need to be written in clear and nonjudgmental language. For instance, write, "Your child does not use any outdoor play equipment," instead of, "I think your child has a fear of climbing."

CHAPTER 14: SPEECH AND LANGUAGE DELAYS

Melinda is two and a half years old and fully engaged with teachers in the toddler room. She smiles and reaches out for a familiar caregiver but uses only a few understandable words. She gets frustrated when an adult doesn't understand the need she is expressing, and sometimes she bites in response. She has also bitten a peer who was playing alongside her. Her teacher has been tracking her development for a few weeks and is ready to talk to her parents about developmental concerns.

Defining Speech and Language Delays

Speech refers to the production of sounds that make words. Language is the meaning assigned to the sounds people use to communicate. Speech and language development begins in infancy, when babies start to coo and then babble. Speech and language differences are common in young children, as each child develops at a unique pace within a range of typical milestones. Some children have an extensive vocabulary by age two, and others use only a handful of words at the same age. Here are some facts to remember about speech and language delays:

- Speech and language delays are the most common type of childhood developmental disabilities.

- Speech and language delays can signal other types of developmental disabilities, so it is important to act early when there are indications of a delay.

- Speech and language therapy early in a child's life can greatly improve speech and language development.

There are three types of speech and language disorders:

Articulation Articulation disorders are difficulties or problems with the way children produce sounds and put sounds together. One sound, like *th*, might be missing, or an incorrect sound, like *w*, might be used instead of the correct one, like *r*.

Childhood Apraxia of Speech (CAS) With this disorder, the brain sends incomplete or faulty information to the muscles of the mouth, so that speech is difficult to make. Speech therapy can help children with CAS develop understandable speech (Mayo Clinic 2013).

Dysfluency and Stuttering This disorder refers to interrupted speech often character-ized by repetition of words or sounds, pauses between words, or no speech production. The exact cause of dysfluency is unknown, though there are genetic links. Children who struggle with speech may become anxious and hinder their speech production more because of tension.

Characteristics of Children with Speech and Language Delay: Implications for Child Care

Speech and language development is vital to a young child's ability to communicate with others in expressing needs, making friends, and finding out about the world. Children need both expressive and receptive language skills, which begin in infancy and continue to develop throughout early childhood.

Expressive language is the ability to communicate to others using language:

- Expressive language is the words children use.

- Expressive language is more difficult than receptive language and comes later for most children.

- If children have difficulty expressing their needs or wants, it can be very frustrating for them.

- Children who are not being understood may use behaviors like biting to get the attention of peers or adults.

- For young children, lack of expressive language can interfere in their early relation-ships, as the give-and-take of responsive caregiving depends on adults tuning in to the expressed needs of infants and toddlers. Nurturing and responsive care means that a child expresses a want or need ("I'm hungry"), and the caregiver responds to meet the need ("I'm getting you a cracker"). Children learn to depend on a caregiver who consis-tently meets their expressed needs.

Receptive language is the ability to listen to and understand language. Here are some important concepts to remember about receptive language:

- Receptive language is the words a child understands.

- Babies respond to their primary caregivers' smiles and soft words by cooing back or turning their head. This represents the beginning of receptive language.

- Communication is very difficult if a child cannot decipher the words being used to convey a message or cannot understand the meaning.

- A child who does not follow directions may seem noncompliant to adults, but if a recep-tive language delay exists, the child may not know what the directions mean.

- Lack of receptive language may cause adults to see challenging behaviors, such as not picking up at cleanup time, when in fact the child may not be aware of the adult's expressed expectations.

When children lack speech and language skills or experience delays, behavior challenges may emerge if delays are not readily recognized. A toddler who cannot tell a peer, "No!" might choose to push instead. Observing and recording all development, including speech and language, can give important clues about the reason for challenging behaviors and indicate where a delay may be present.

Red Flags for Speech and Language Disorders

Most children who are typically developing will have speech irregularities as they develop early speech. Language is complex, as is the ability to communicate. Young children are not always able to keep up with the rapid expression of their thoughts through their current language skills, so we see children skip words or leave out syllables as they eagerly tell us something. It becomes a concern when milestones are missed beyond a typical range, or when regression of development is seen.

Red flags for speech and language concerns include the following signs:

In Infants

- No babbling

- Older baby babbling but not imitating caregiver sounds

- No smiling or interaction

- No response to sounds

- No response to name

- No startle reaction to loud sounds

- Twelve-month-old using no words

- No laughing or squealing

In Toddlers

- No words by age two

- No pointing to show things

- Inability to point to a familiar object when asked

- No imitation of words

- No two-word sentences

- No following simple directions

- Lack of understanding of what others say

- No sounds for common animals (cat, dog, cow, and so on)

In Preschoolers

- Speech that is hard to understand, even for familiar caregivers

- Abnormalities in voice quality, such as monotone, high pitch, or low pitch

- Frequent ear infections

- Challenges playing with peers

- No engagement in pretend or dramatic play

- No answer to questions such as why, what, and who

- Lack of response when spoken to

- Not seeming to understand others

- Inability to follow two- or three-step directions

- Regression in speech skills

Speech and language delays can be part of other disabilities, such as autism, cerebral palsy, traumatic brain injury, cleft palate, and other physical and neurological disorders. If you suspect a delay, keep the following in mind:

- Children whose speech and language delay are identified early can often make great gains in development.

- A speech and language pathologist will create a plan for speech therapy, which can be integrated into home and child care.

- Sharing strategies among professionals is a key to better outcomes for the young child. To talk to specialists working with a child in their care, child care providers need written permission from parents or guardians.

Practical Application: Supporting the Development of Children with Speech and Language Delay

Many of the strategies for adapting the child care environment to meet the needs of children with speech and language delays are simply good practice. From infants to preschoolers, young children are learning language by hearing it in multiple ways. For a child with a delay, having a language-rich environment will assist speech acquisition.

The child care setting can be a rich source of opportunities for promoting language in infants, toddlers, and preschoolers. Responsive care of infants means tuning in to their needs as they express unhappiness because they are hungry or express joy because a person to whom they are attached is smiling at them. Toddlers eagerly chant, "Me!" when it is time for snack or a favorite toy. Preschoolers pretend in dramatic play to be doctors, firefighters, moms, and dads while conversing with peers. The environment should be set up in a way that encourages interaction among peers as well as among children and adults. Following are some strategies:

Environment

- Encourage small-group and partner-play opportunities.

- Keep noise levels down.

- Get down at the children's level to talk to them.

- Allow children to share stories and listen to one another during group time.

- Use natural boundaries like shelving to break up large areas into smaller activity centers.

- Design the room so quiet areas are next to one another, away from louder activity areas.

- Be aware of noise levels in your program. Watch for sensory overload from sounds that could make listening more difficult.

- Keep distractions to a minimum.

- Ensure that your environment is print rich, with books of all sizes. Encourage children to hold and touch books.

- Read, read, and read some more. Help families understand the importance of reading to their children.

- Use story time to teach language as well as to give children opportunities to share thoughts about stories. Use a listening prop so each child has time to finish talking without interruption.

- Label play materials and activity areas with both words and pictures.

- Say the names of the play centers frequently to everyone. For example, "Who's going to the art center?" Or, "What are you making with the blue and red blocks?"

- Use a visual schedule that includes written words and pictures of the activities of the day. Refer to it when changing events. Tell children what is happening next.

- Help a child express feelings with a feelings cube or feelings wheel that has pictures and words for emotions.

- Use visual cue cards that show steps to complete a task or that show when transitions are occurring. The cards should have pictures and words.

- For preschoolers, consider having listening centers with audio recordings and headphones to encourage other kinds of storytelling or listening activities.

- Spend one-on-one time with a child who has language delays. Be intentional in engaging with the child through language.

- Sing songs and use rhyming. Make words fun. Be patient!

In addition to having an environment that supports language skill development, the interactions between a child and teacher and between peers also assist language acquisition. Here are some strategies for building speech and language skills through relationships:

Relationships and Interactions

- Pair a child who has a delay with a peer who has strong language skills as part of a planned play period.

- Have peers model language through different activities to help a child with a delay understand language usage.

- Have a teacher model understanding and encouragement to a child with a speech and language delay to promote an atmosphere of belonging and acceptance.

- Talk to children during daily routines, starting in infancy. Describe what is going on around them. Teachers should talk to babies during diaper changes, not to other adults in the room. Describe to a toddler what others in the room are doing.

- With preschoolers, connect words to actions. For example, "Let's walk. You are moving your feet and legs. That is called walking."

- Give children words for what they are playing with and engaging in. Expand their vocabulary. For example, tell them, "You chose the yellow car," or, "You and Jimmy are firefighters."

- Get at the children's level when speaking to them. Speak more slowly and more distinctly.

- Engage children in speech in their own interest areas. For instance, if a child likes cars, talk to the child about the color of a car, the sound it might make, and where it goes.

- Look for opportunities to expand and extend children's expressed ideas. For instance, if children say they made a blue dragon, you can say, "What else is blue?" or, "Blue is the color of the sky during the day. What color is the sky at night?"

- Avoid correcting speech sounds as a child is talking. Simply say sounds correctly when you talk to the child. For example, if children struggle with *th* sounds, let them say "this" in their own way, but as you speak back, use the correct pronunciation.

- If a child is nonverbal, learn the communication system the family and therapists are incorporating. If signing is the child's communication method, help all the children in the program learn some simple signs for common words or phrases.

- Model acceptance and understanding of everyone, regardless of needs.

Strategies that encourage speech and language skill development for a child with a speech delay, like describing what the child is doing while the child is doing it, will benefit all children in a child care program during the first few years of life. Children are acquiring speech and language skills from infancy, whether they are typically or atypically developing. A high-quality early childhood program promotes language and speech through its environment, activities, and responsive interactions.

CHAPTER 15: PUTTING IT ALL TOGETHER

Monica has been enrolled in her community child care program from infancy. She is twenty-six months old and has recently been diagnosed with developmental delays that include motor delays. The staff observed and recorded her ongoing development, recognizing red flags when Monica was not crawling at ten months. Teachers shared concerns with her parents and helped them by making a referral to the local early intervention program, where she was evaluated. Since then, the staff and family have worked closely with therapists and special educators to ensure that Monica continues to progress in her development.

Having knowledge of various disabilities is helpful to early educators, because this knowledge provides a starting place from which to meet a child's needs. Each child is unique, and the impact of a disability is different for each child. Many adaptations for one disability are good practice for other disabilities as well—and for children who are typically developing.

Ensuring Confidentiality

It is important to remember the importance of confidentiality when you are working with children who have disabilities. Keep in mind the following guidelines:

Medical information about a child is protected by federal law. In a classroom, disability information should be provided on a need-to-know basis. Children's disability and health records should be kept secure. No records should be accessible to the entire staff. Never discuss one child's special needs with other families or children.

No information about a child or family should be shared externally without the parents' or legal guardians' written consent. Signed information releases are not required in the case of suspected child abuse, neglect, or maltreatment, since child care professionals are mandated reporters.

Families should be told upon enrollment that a program has strict confidentiality procedures. This reassurance supports a trusting relationship with families.

Confidential or proprietary documentation and information must be disposed of in a secure manner. Shredding of personal information ensures that children's identities are protected once they leave the program or once the information is outdated or replaced.

Confidentiality and protection of data privacy applies to both written and oral exchanges. Conversations about people receiving services should occur only in the work environment and only when required and necessary in the provision of services.

Supporting Families and Other Professionals

Inclusion is most effective when everyone is working together to build successful outcomes for children with special needs. Parents or guardians, educators, and other professionals need to make sure their relationships meet the following criteria:

Relationships are built on a foundation of trust. Parents or guardians need to provide written consent for sharing information across agencies. Families need to know that their children's personal and medical data will not be shared with anyone who does not have permission. Educators and other professionals need to ensure they do not talk negatively about anyone involved to one another, to families, or to other professionals.

Relationships are supported by effective communication. It's important to talk about expectations, goals, and strategies for achieving specific outcomes. Written communication back and forth can keep everyone clear on progress. Use whatever tools work best for the team working with a particular child.

Relationships promote mutual respect and understanding of each person's role. Everyone brings expertise to the table. No one person's role is more important than that of another. Parents are children's first teachers, and they know their children best. Parents need to know that their feelings and their ideas about their children's goals are respected. Professionals who provide therapy and services bring specific types of expertise that are crucial to children's early intervention success. Child care providers have a knowledge of children that is unique to early education settings. All of these people play important roles in helping children achieve the best outcomes.

Inclusion Works

Children are children, regardless of ability. They all need to grow across developmental domains. Most importantly, they all need to belong to caring and nurturing communities that support their unique learning needs.

Inclusion of a child with a special need means having tools in place to be successful, a supportive team of specialists who know what therapies will be most effective, and a strong relationship with the family to know what a child does when away from child care. Inclusion works because people make it work.

RESOURCES

American Speech-Language-Hearing Association (ASHA)
www.asha.org

Center for Inclusive Child Care (CICC)
www.inclusivechildcare.org

Children and Youth with Special Health Needs (CYSHN)
www.health.state.mn.us/cyshn

Commonly Asked Questions about Child Care Centers and the Americans with Disabilities Act
www.ada.gov/childqanda.htm

Early Childhood Technical Assistance (ECTA) Center
ectacenter.org

Fraser
www.fraser.org

Learn the Signs. Act Early.
www.cdc.gov/ncbddd/actearly/index.html

Mental Health Information
www.nimh.nih.gov/health/topics

Minnesota Association for Children's Mental Health (MACMH)
www.macmh.org

National Down Syndrome Society (NDSS)
www.ndss.org

PACER Center
www.pacer.org

United Cerebral Palsy (UCP)
ucp.org

Universal Design for Learning (UDL)
accessproject.colostate.edu/udl

GLOSSARY OF TERMS

adaptive equipment: any device used to assist with activities of daily living and to increase independence

American Sign Language (ASL): a visual and gestural language with its own words and syntax

Americans with Disabilities Act (ADA): a comprehensive civil rights law passed in 1990 to protect people with disabilities from discrimination

articulation: the production of speech sounds

assistive technology: any item, piece of equipment, or product system, whether acquired commercially, off the shelf, modified, or customized, that is used to increase, maintain, or improve functional capabilities of individuals with disabilities

atypical development: any aspect of a child's physical or psychological makeup that is different from what is generally accepted as typical

audiologist: a certified professional who conducts hearing testing with specialized equipment

autism spectrum disorder (ASD): a neurological disorder that interferes with a child's ability to communicate and interact with others

cerebral palsy (CP): a brain-based muscular condition affecting muscle tone, reflexes, movement, and motor development

cochlear implant: a surgical treatment for hearing loss that sends electrical stimuli directly to the auditory nerve in the ear. A cochlear implant is different from a hearing aid, which simply amplifies sound.

cued speech: system of visual communication that uses handshapes and placements in combination with the mouth movements of speech to make the sounds of a spoken language look different from one another

developmentally appropriate practice (DAP): an approach to teaching grounded in the research on how young children develop and learn and in what is known about effective early education. Its framework is designed to promote young children's optimal learning and development.

developmental delay: when a child does not meet developmental milestones at the expected time

developmental milestone: an achievement or ability, such as sitting, crawling, walking, or language acquisition, that has special importance in the growth, motor functioning, or social development of infants, toddlers, and older children and teens, usually associated with a particular age range

developmental red flags: behavioral or developmental signs suggesting the need for further evaluation

Down syndrome: a genetic disorder that occurs when a person has an extra chromosome in the twenty-first pair. There are three types of Down syndrome: trisomy 21, translocation pattern, and mosaic pattern.

dysregulation: the failure to properly regulate metabolically, physiologically, or psychologically

expressive language: the ability to communicate to others using language

expulsion: the practice of disenrolling a child from a child care program or education setting with no intention of readmittance

fine-motor skills: movement of smaller muscles, such as in the hands, fingers, feet, and toes

floor time: a five-step process of interacting with a child or group of children that allows adults to be aware of and build on their intuitive understanding of a child's emotional needs for growth

formal assessments: evaluations conducted by professionals with expertise in both typical and atypical development. Expertise may include specialized training in psychology, special education, speech and language therapy, occupational or physical therapy, social work, nursing, or other health-related fields.

goodness of fit: how the child care environment works together with a child's temperament and learning needs to produce favorable outcomes for the child. Goodness of fit recognizes each child's unique personality while helping the child function more adaptively.

gross-motor skills: movement of the larger muscles, such as those in the trunk, neck, arms, and legs

handling: preparation of child for movement and positioning. Handling depends on muscle tone and reflex.

hard of hearing: partial loss of hearing. It can be mild, moderate, or severe.

hypertonic: having high muscle tone, or muscles that are tense and spastic

hypotonic: having low muscle tone, or muscles that have low tension, which makes it difficult to maintain control of posture

informal assessments: evaluations that generally occur in the child's family child care or preschool setting and are made by professionals who work with the child on a regular basis. These assessments occur over time and in a variety of settings.

inclusion: holding high expectations for children with disabilities and intentionally promoting their participation in all learning and social activities, facilitated by individualized accommodations. Inclusion uses evidence-based services and supports to foster their development (cognitive, language, communication, physical, behavioral, and social-emotional), friendships with peers, and sense of belonging.

Individuals with Disabilities Education Act (IDEA): a federal law that protects the educational rights of children with disabilities and guarantees a free and appropriate public education (FAPE)

least restrictive environment (LRE): a principle holding that a student who has a disability should have the opportunity to be educated with peers who do not have disabilities, to the greatest extent appropriate under the law

midline crossing: the ability of a body part, such as a foot or hand, to spontaneously move over to the other side of the body to work there

muscle tone: the degree of tension in a muscle when it is at rest

natural setting or environment: a setting that is natural or typical for a same-age infant or toddler without a disability (may include the home or community settings)

neurotoxin: a poisonous agent or substance that inhibits, damages, or destroys the tissues of the nervous system, especially neurons, the conducting cells of the body's central nervous system

nonambulatory: unable to walk without mechanical assistance (using a wheelchair, crutches, or other assistive devices)

perseveration: repetition of a word, action, or gesture insistently or redundantly

positioning: how a child's specific motor and reflex needs are met by careful placement and support of the child's body

profoundly deaf: unable to detect sound, even at the highest volume

readily achievable: a term under the ADA that means easily accomplishable without much difficulty or expense

receptive language: the ability to listen and understand language

sensory processing: the brain's ability to receive information through the senses and interpret that information throughout the day to learn, function, and survive

sensory processing disorder (SPD): the brain's inability to process sensory information. Some describe it as misfiring in the brain.

speech and language delays: difficulties in the production of words and the processing of language to communicate

typical development: the process of growing, changing, and acquiring a range of skills at approximately the same age and in the same sequence as the majority of children do

undue burden: a term under the ADA that means significant difficulty or expense

universal design for learning (UDL): a set of principles and techniques for creating inclusive classroom instruction and accessible course materials. At its core is the assertion that *all* students benefit when they are given multiples ways to take in new information, express their comprehension, and become engaged in learning.

REFERENCES

Allen, K. Eileen, and Glynnis E. Cowdery. 2012. *The Exceptional Child: Inclusion in Early Childhood Education*. 7th ed. Belmont, CA: Wadsworth, Cengage Learning.

American Speech-Language-Hearing Association (ASHA). 2016. "Early Detection of Speech, Language, and Hearing Disorders." Accessed April 5. www.asha.org/public/Early -Detection-of-Speech-Language-and-Hearing-Disorders.

Americans with Disabilities Act (ADA) of 1990, as Amended. June 15, 2009. www.ada.gov /pubs/adastatute08.htm.

Anxiety and Depression Association of America (ADAA). 2015. "Childhood Anxiety Disorders." www.adaa.org/living-with-anxiety/children/childhood-anxiety-disorders.

Bentley, Chris. 2005. *Inclusion in Child Care: A Manual for Consultants*. Richfield, MN: Fraser.

Berk, Laura E. 2013. *Child Development*. 9th ed. Upper Saddle River, NJ: Pearson Education.

Berk, Laura E., and Adam Winsler. 1995. *Scaffolding Children's Learning: Vygotsky and Early Childhood Education*. Washington, DC: NAEYC.

Buysse, Virginia, Barbara Davis Goldman, and Martie Skinner. 2002. "Setting Effects on Friendship Formation among Young Children with and without Disabilities." *Exceptional Children*. 68 (4): 503–517.

Center for Inclusive Child Care. 2011. *Project EXCEPTIONAL MN: A Guide for Training and Recruiting Child Care Providers to Serve Young Children with Disabilities*. Saint Paul, MN: Center for Inclusive Child Care.

Center for Inclusive Child Care. 2011. "What Is Autism?" www.inclusivechildcare.org/pdf /Autism%20Tip%20Sheet.pdf.

Center for Inclusive Child Care. 2014. "How to Prevent Disenrollment in Child Care." www .inclusivechildcare.org/pdf/Disenrollment_Tip_Sheet_Oct%202014.pdf.

Center for Inclusive Child Care. 2015. "Developmental Delay." www.inclusivechildcare.org.

Center for Inclusive Child Care. 2016. "CICC Tip Sheets." Accessed April 12. www .inclusivechildcare.org/tipsheets.cfm.

Center for Inclusive Child Care. 2016. "Online Self-Study Courses." Accessed April 12. www .inclusivechildcare.org/learning-self-study.cfm.

Centers for Disease Control and Prevention (CDC). 2015. "Hearing Loss in Children." www
.cdc.gov/ncbddd/hearingloss/facts.html.

Centers for Disease Control and Prevention (CDC). 2016. "Autism Spectrum Disorder (ASD)."
www.cdc.gov/ncbddd/autism/facts.html.

Child Care Law Center. 2011. "United States Department of Justice ADA Settlement
Summaries." http://childcarelaw.org/wp-content/uploads/2014/06/DOJ-ADA-Settlement
-Summaries.pdf.

Child Mind Institute. 2015. "Children's Mental Health Report." http://speakupforkids.org
/ChildrensMentalHealthReport_052015.pdf.

Collins Dictionary. 2016. "Profoundly Deaf." Accessed April 12. www.collinsdictionary.com
/dictionary/english/profoundly-deaf.

Croft, Cindy. 2007. *The Six Keys: Promoting Children's Mental Health in Early Childhood
Programs*. Farmington, MN: Sparrow Media Group.

DEC/NAEYC. 2009. *Early Childhood Inclusion: A Joint Position Statement of the Division for
Early Childhood (DEC) and the National Association for the Education of Young Children
(NAEYC)*. Chapel Hill: The University of North Carolina, FPG Child Development Institute.

Farlex, Inc. 2016. "Medical Dictionary." Accessed April 12. http://medical-dictionary
.thefreedictionary.com.

Gilliam, Walter S. 2008. "Implementing Policies to Reduce the Likelihood of Preschool
Expulsion." *Foundation for Child Development, A. L. Mailman Family Foundation, and
Schott Foundation for Public Education*. http://ziglercenter.yale.edu/publications
/PreKExpulsionBrief2_tcm350-34772_tcm350-284-32.pdf.

Mayo Clinic. 2013. "Childhood Apraxia of Speech." www.mayoclinic.org/diseases-conditions
/childhood-apraxia-of-speech/basics/definition/con-20031147.

Minnesota Association for Children's Mental Health (MACMH). 2016. "Children's Mental
Health Disorder Fact Sheet for the Classroom: Anxiety Disorders." Accessed April 1. www
.macmh.org/publications/fact_sheets/Anxiety.pdf.

Minnesota Organization on Fetal Alcohol Syndrome (MOFAS). 2010. "FASD Screening and
Diagnosis." www.mofas.org/2014/05/fasd-screening-and-diagnosis.

National Cued Speech Association (NCSA). 2016. "Cuedspeech.org." Accessed April 12. www
.cuedspeech.org.

National Down Syndrome Society (NDSS). 2016. "What Is Down Syndrome?" Accessed April
12. www.ndss.org/Down-Syndrome/What-Is-Down-Syndrome.

National Institute of Mental Health (NIMH). 2016. "Generalized Anxiety Disorder among
Children." Accessed April 12. www.nimh.nih.gov/health/statistics/prevalence
/generalized-anxiety-disorder-among-children.shtml.

National Institute of Mental Health (NIMH). 2016. "Mental Health Information." Accessed April 12. www.nimh.nih.gov/health/topics.

National Professional Development Center on Inclusion (NPDCI). 2011. "Research Synthesis Points on Quality Inclusive Practices." Chapel Hill: The University of North Carolina, FPG Child Development Institute. www.researchconnections.org/files/meetings/ccprc/2007/10/10IResearchSynthesisPointsonEarlychildhoodinclusion.pdf.

National Association for the Education of Young Children (NAEYC). 2016. "Developmentally Appropriate Practice (DAP)." Accessed April 12. www.naeyc.org/DAP.

Purcell, Megan L., Eva Horn, and Susan Palmer. 2007. "A Qualitative Study of the Initiation and Continuation of Preschool Inclusion Programs." *Exceptional Children* 74 (1): 85–99.

SPD Foundation. 2016. "About SPD." Accessed April 6. http://spdfoundation.net/about-sensory-processing-disorder.

US Department of Health and Human Services (DHHS) and US Department of Education (DOE). 2014. "Policy Statement on Expulsion and Suspension Policies in Early Childhood Settings." www.acf.hhs.gov/sites/default/files/ecd/expulsion_suspension_final.pdf.

US Department of Health and Human Services (DHHS) and US Department of Education (DOE). 2015. "Policy Statement on Inclusion of Children with Disabilities in Early Childhood Programs: Executive Summary." www2.ed.gov/policy/speced/guid/earlylearning/joint-statement-executive-summary.pdf.

US Department of Justice (DOJ). 1997. "Commonly Asked Questions about Child Care Centers and the Americans with Disabilities Act." www.ada.gov/childqanda.htm.

ABOUT THE AUTHOR

Cindy Croft is the director of the Center for Inclusive Child Care (CICC) at Concordia University in Saint Paul, Minnesota, where she also serves as faculty in the College of Education. She is field faculty at the University of Minnesota's Center for Early Education and Development (CEED) and teaches for the Minnesota online Eager-to-Learn program. She has her master of arts in education, with an emphasis on early childhood. She authored The Six Keys: Strategies for Promoting Children's Mental Health in Early Childhood Programs and coedited Children and Challenging Behavior: Making Inclusion Work with Deborah Hewitt. Croft has worked in the early childhood field for the past twenty-five years.